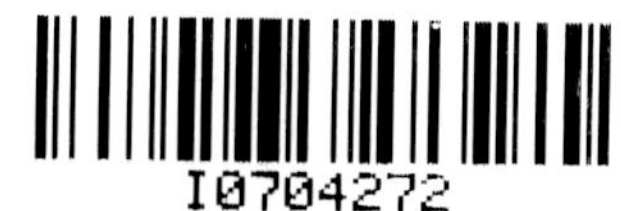

This Book Belongs to:

____

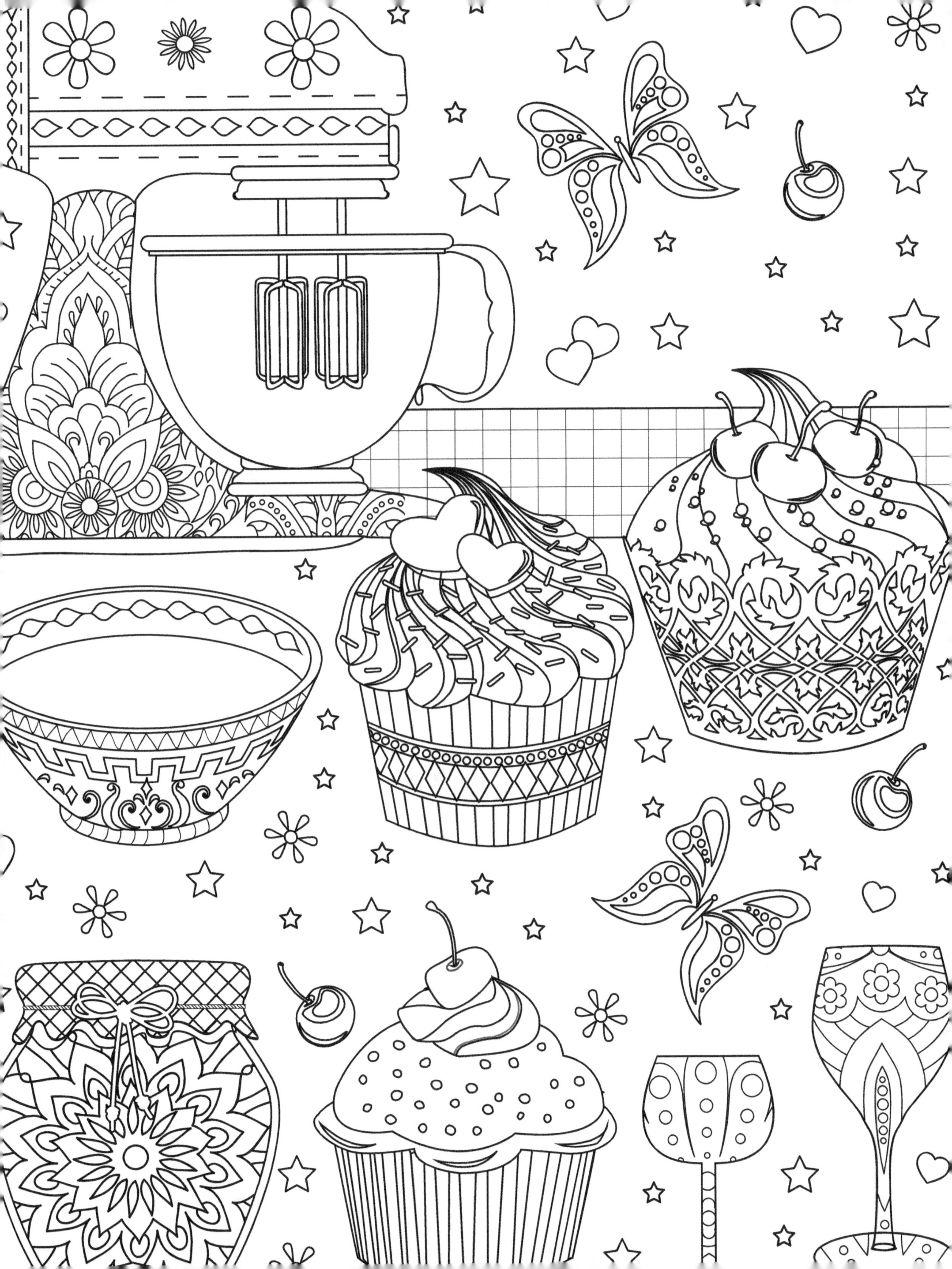

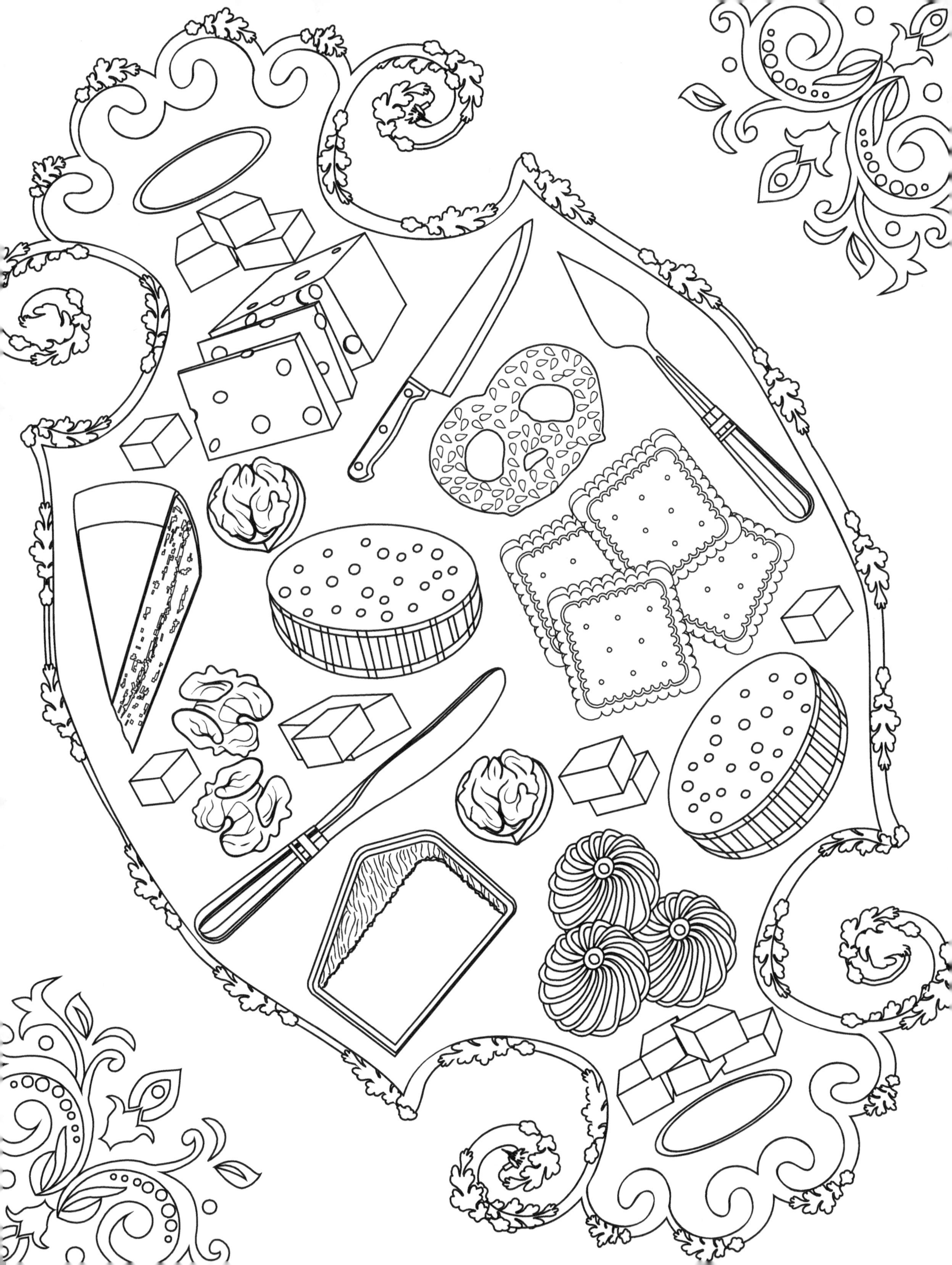

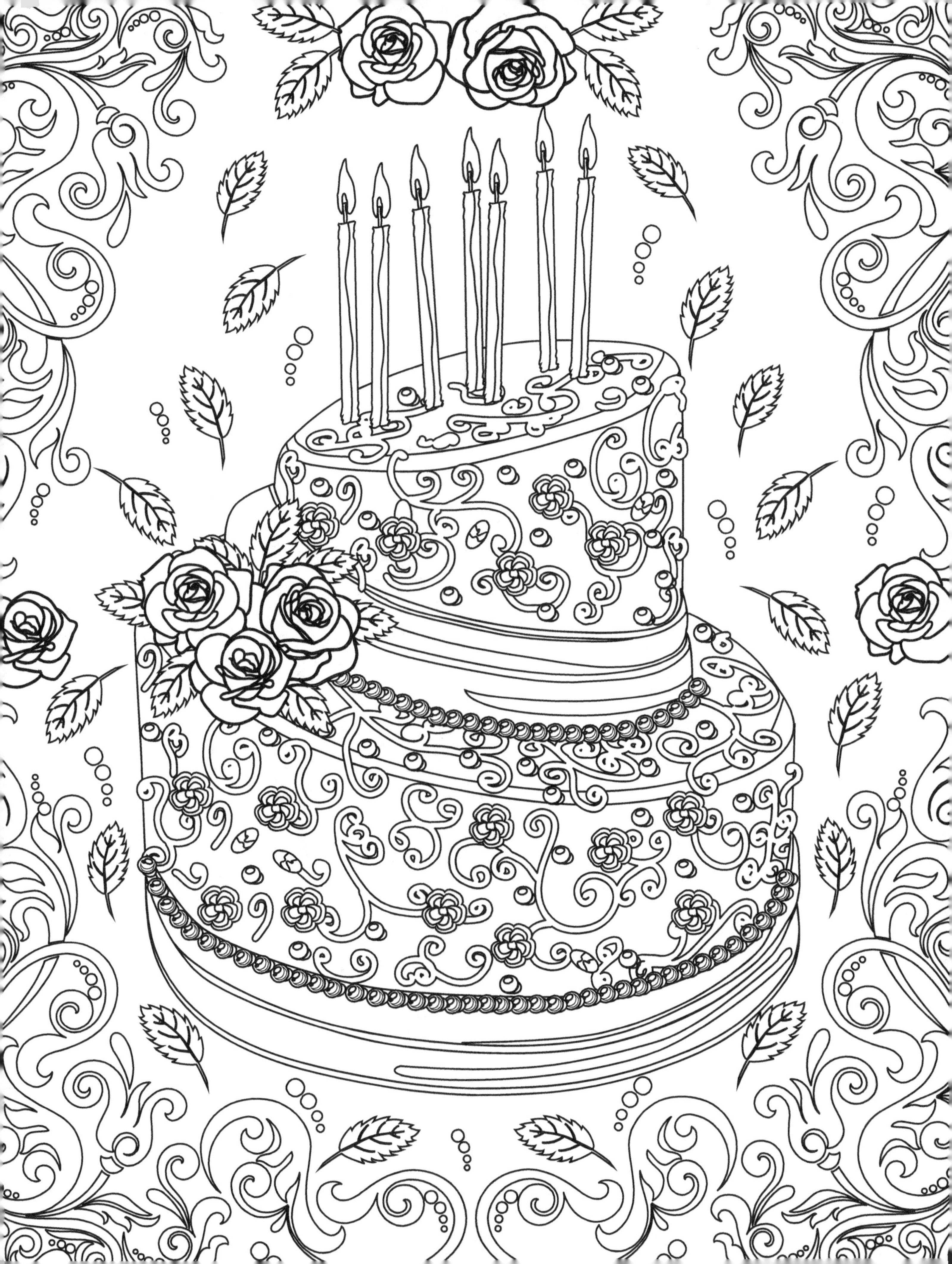

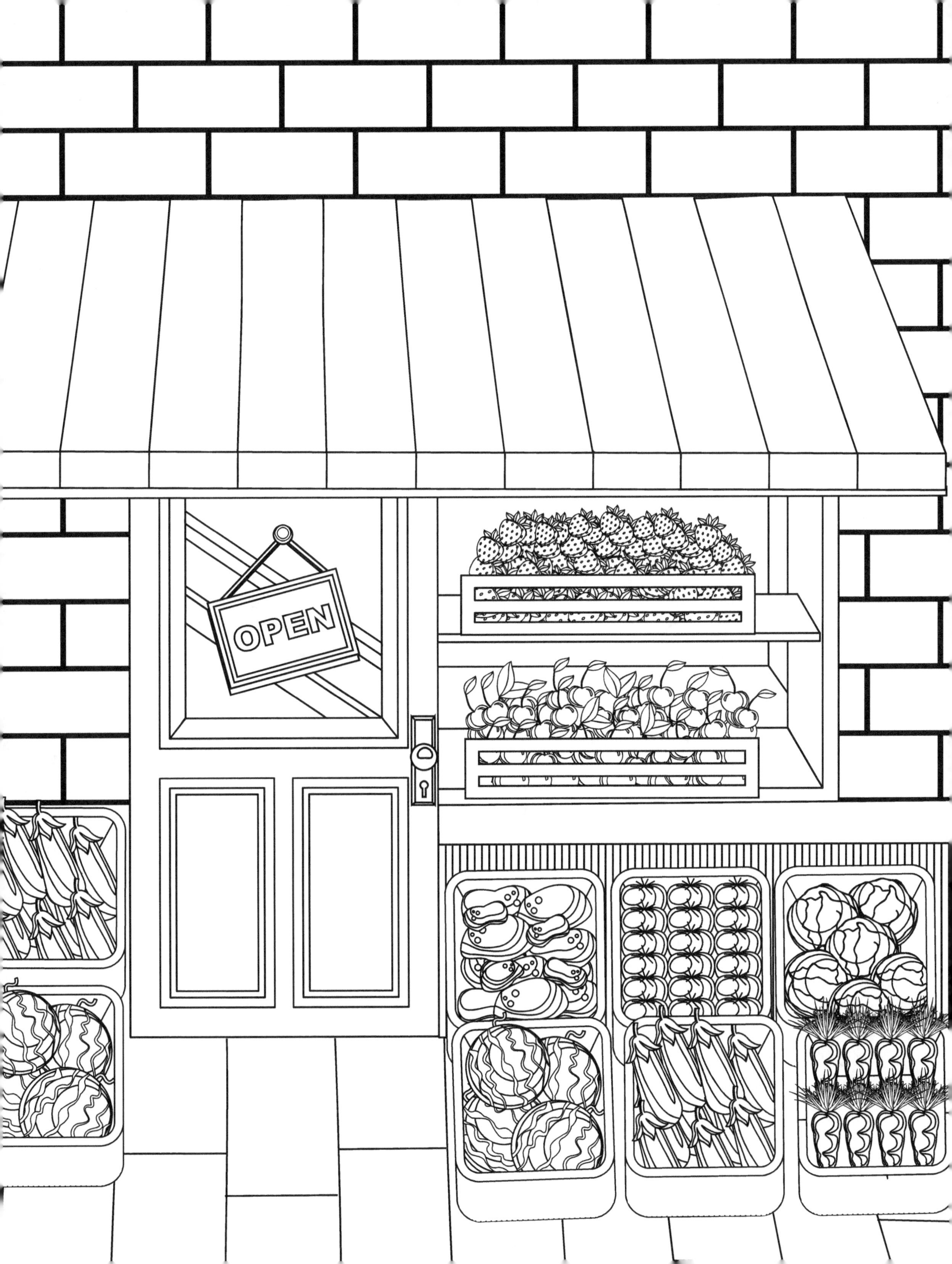

OPEN

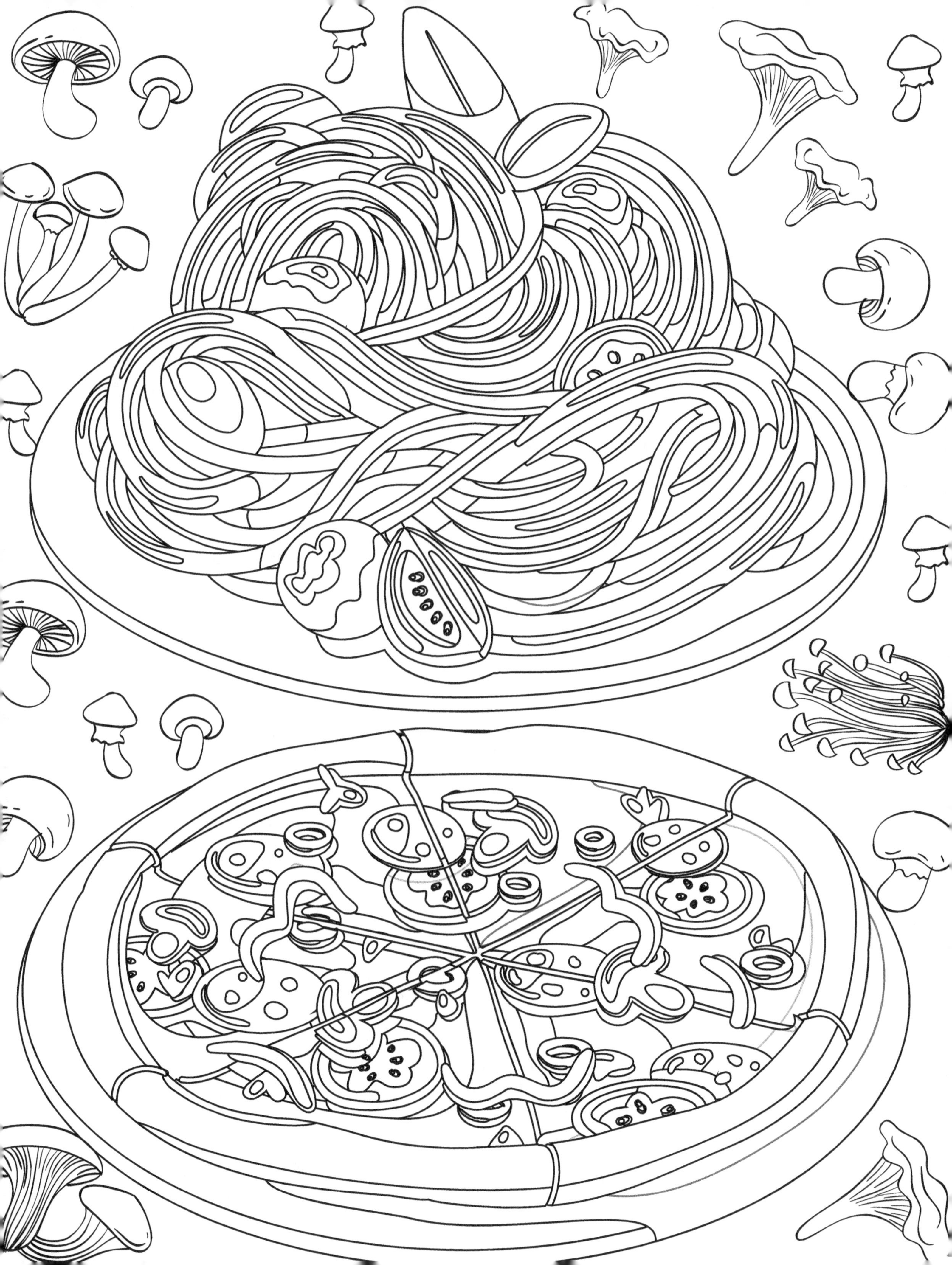

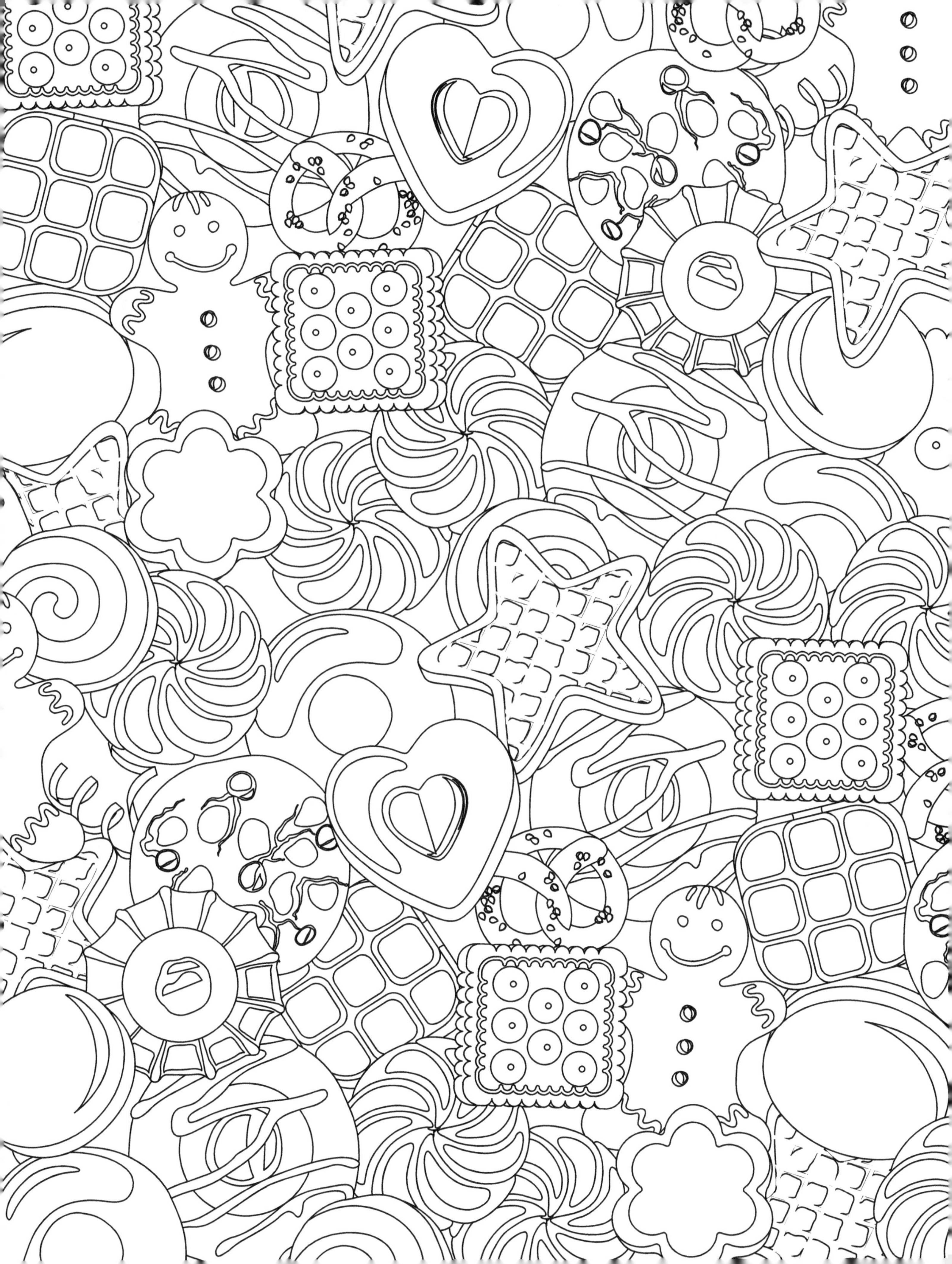

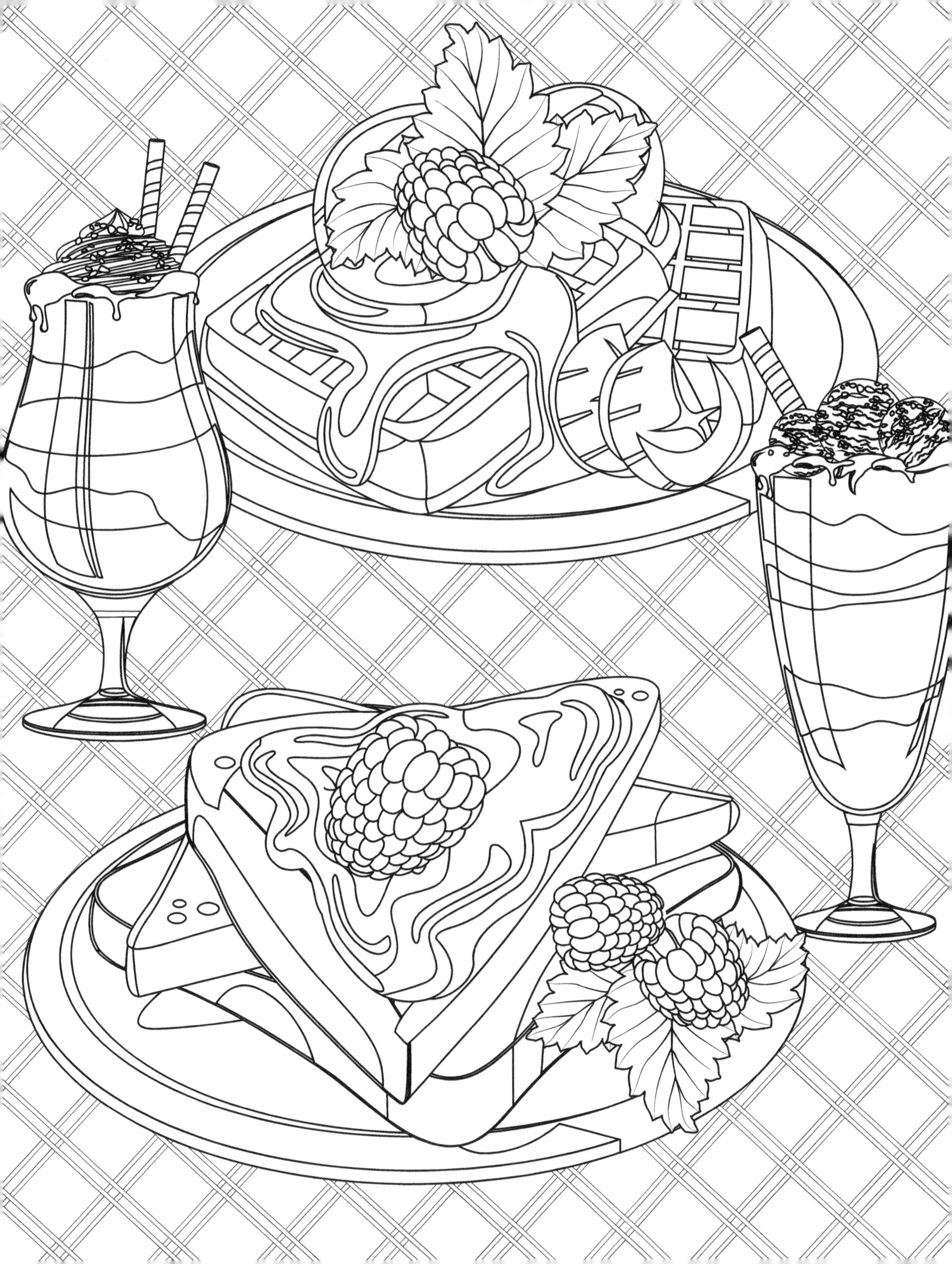

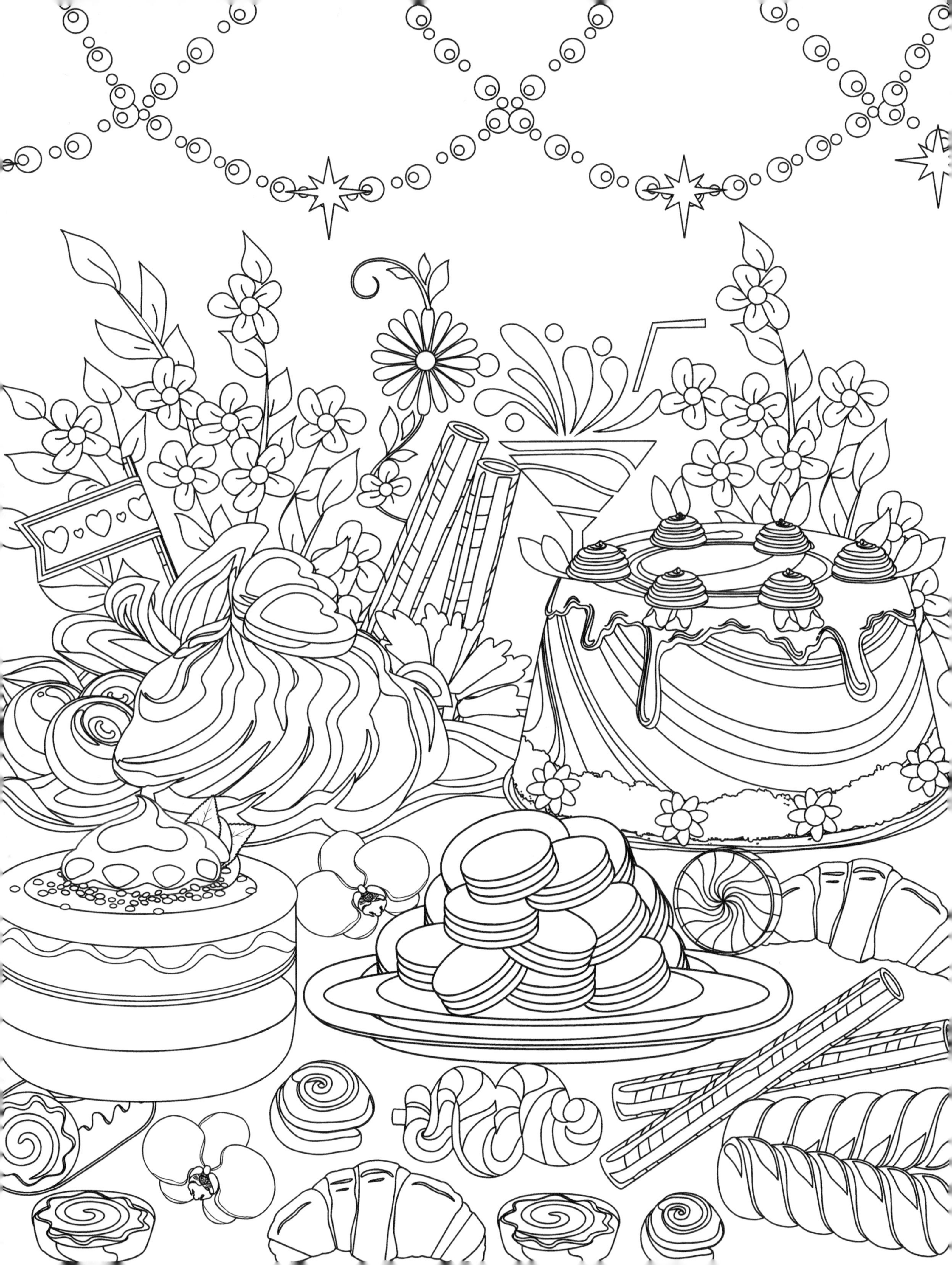

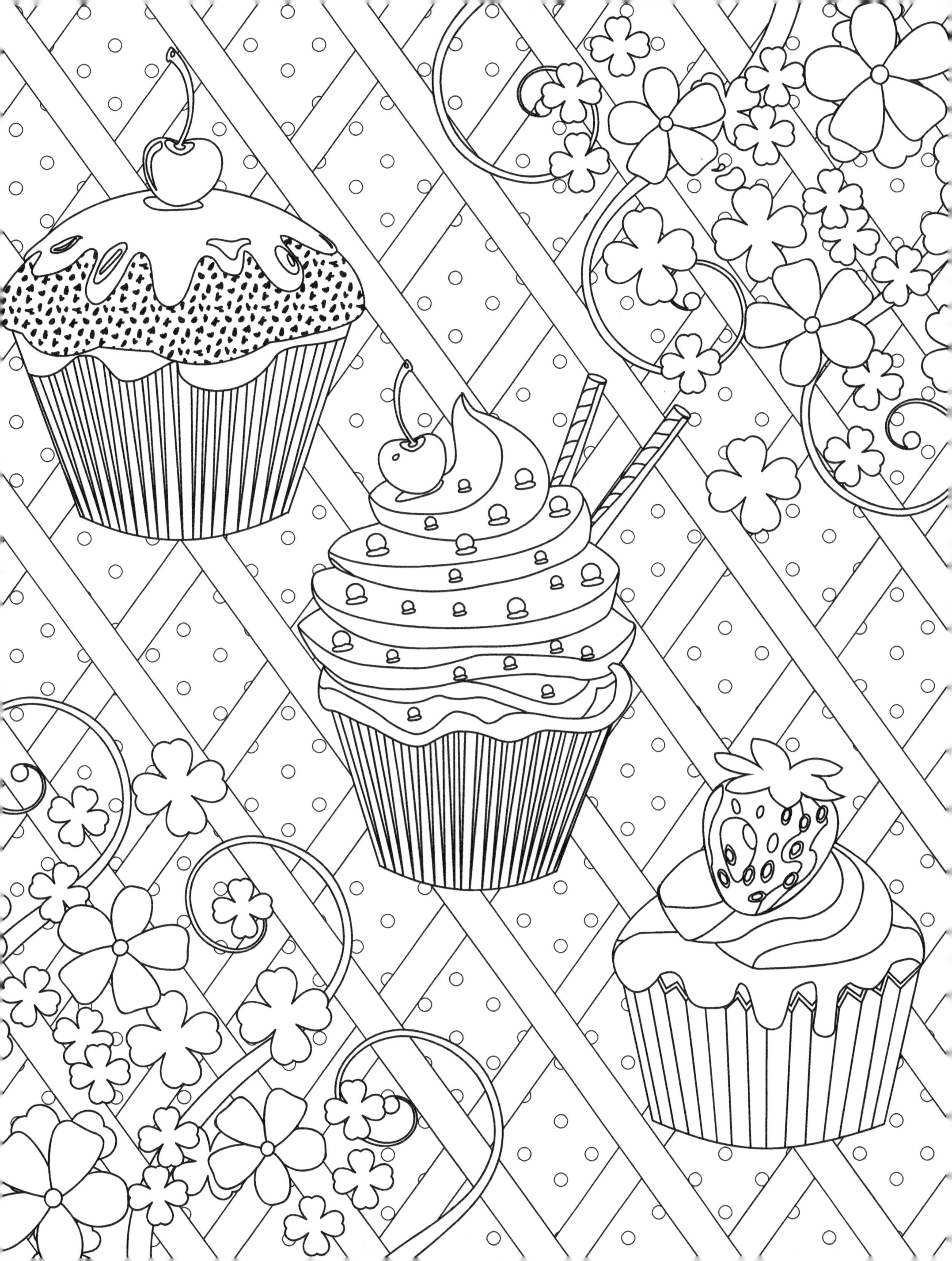

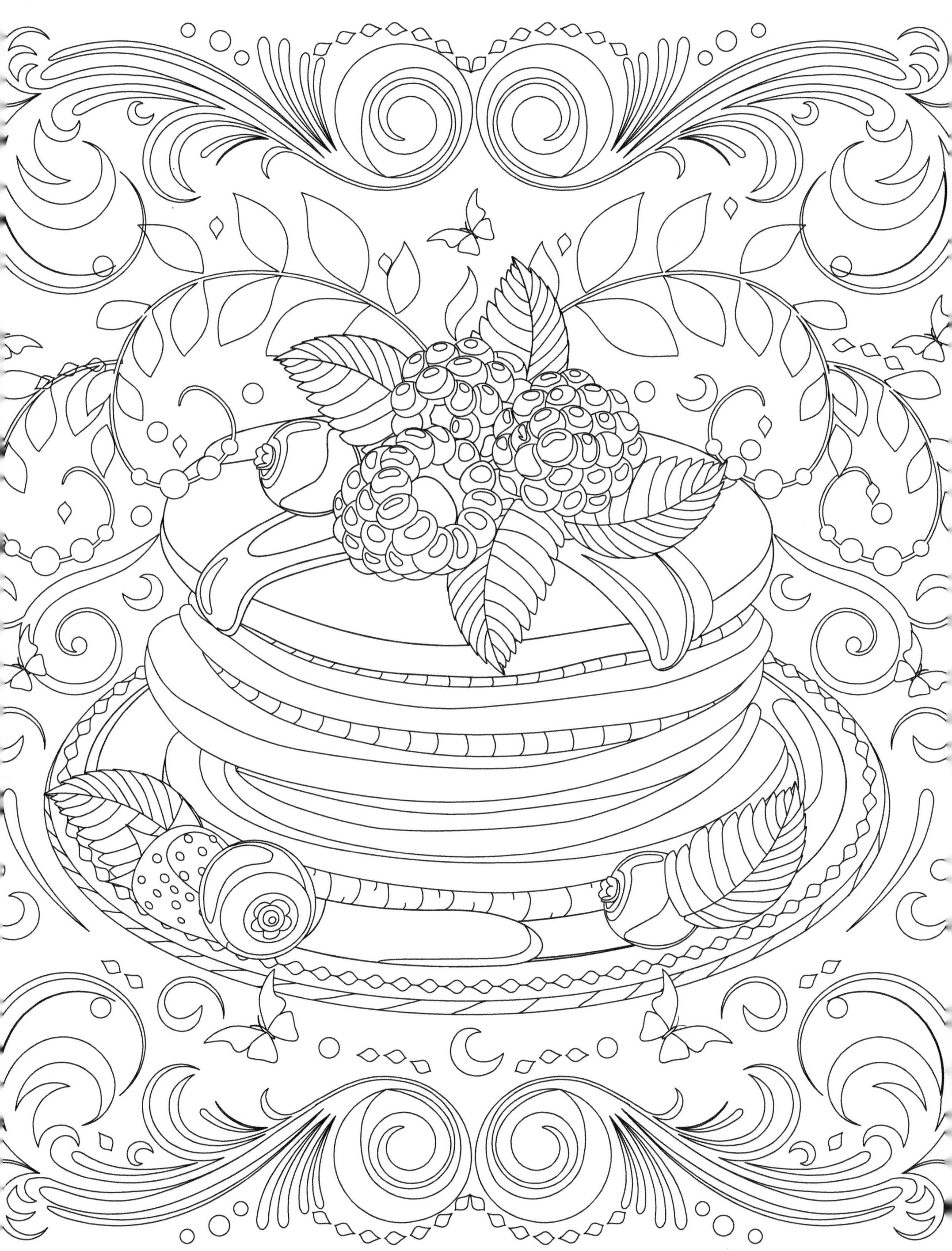

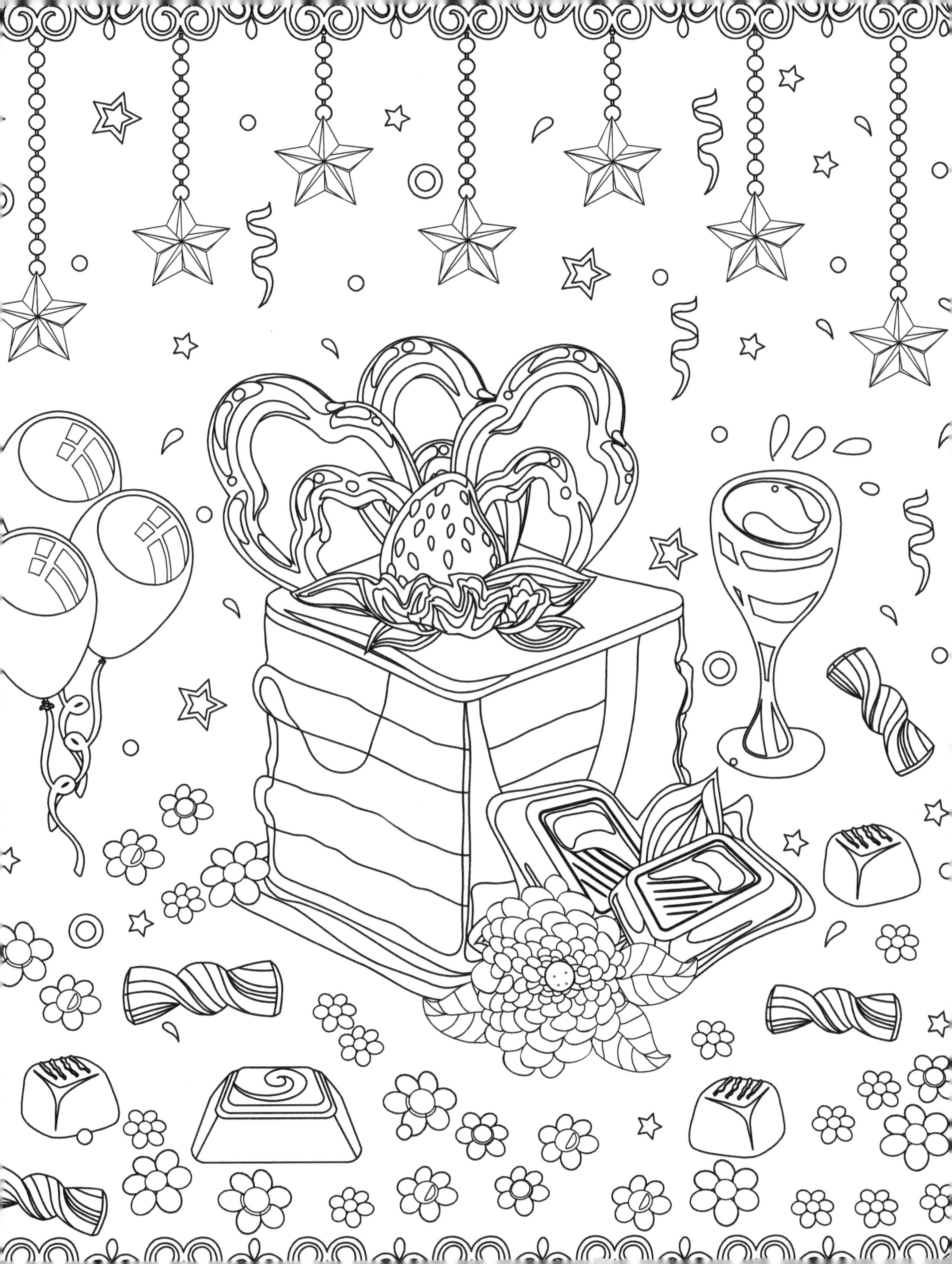

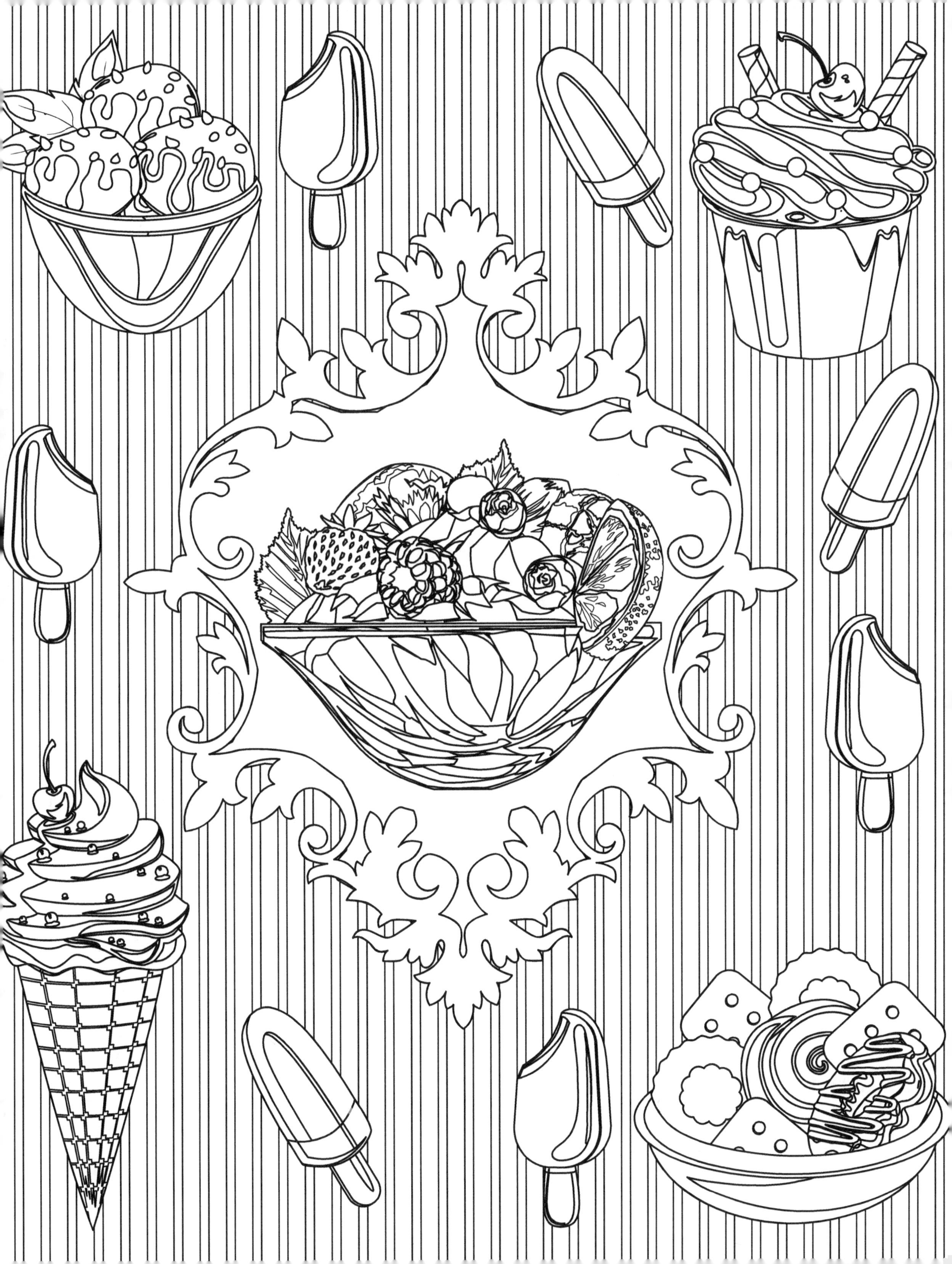

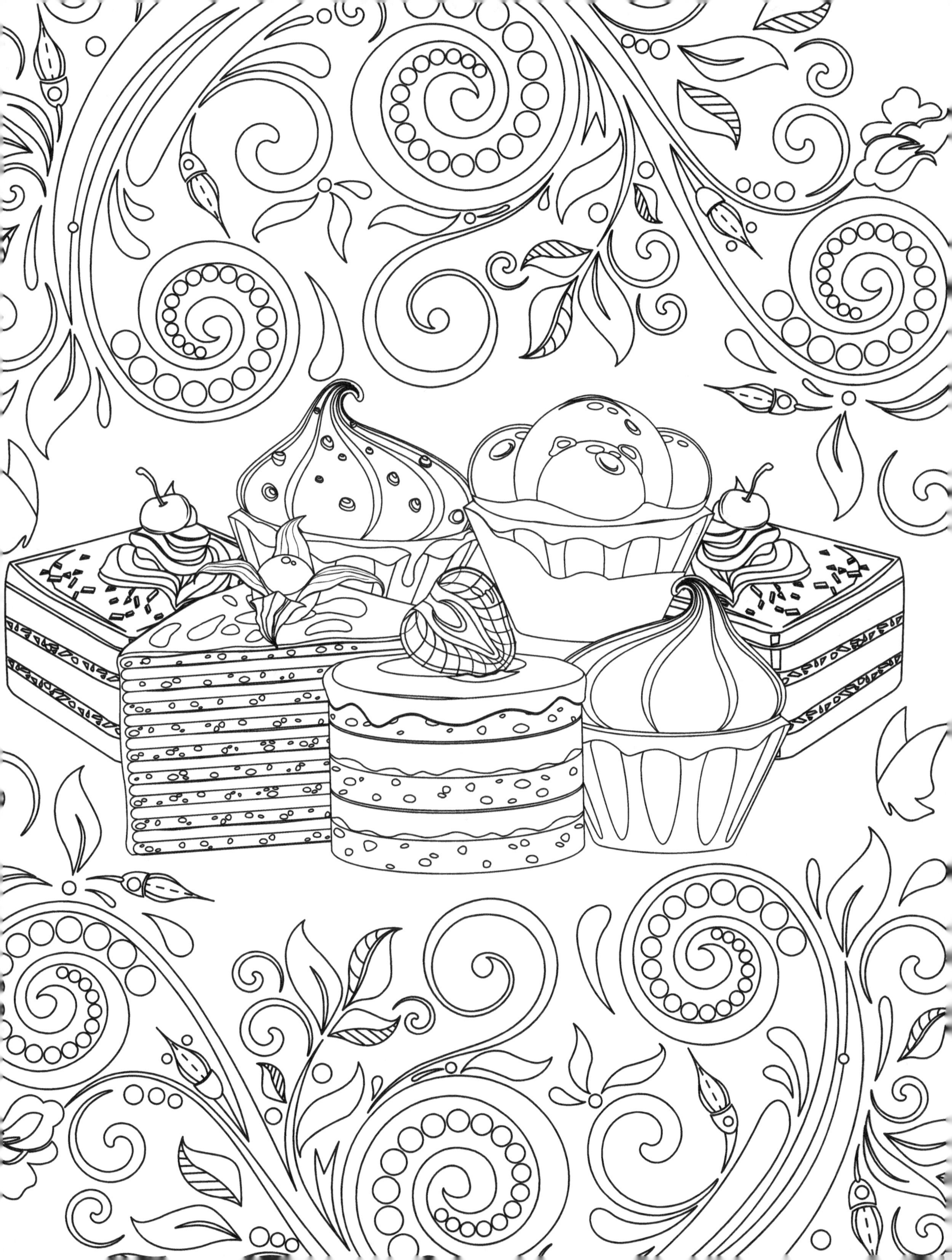

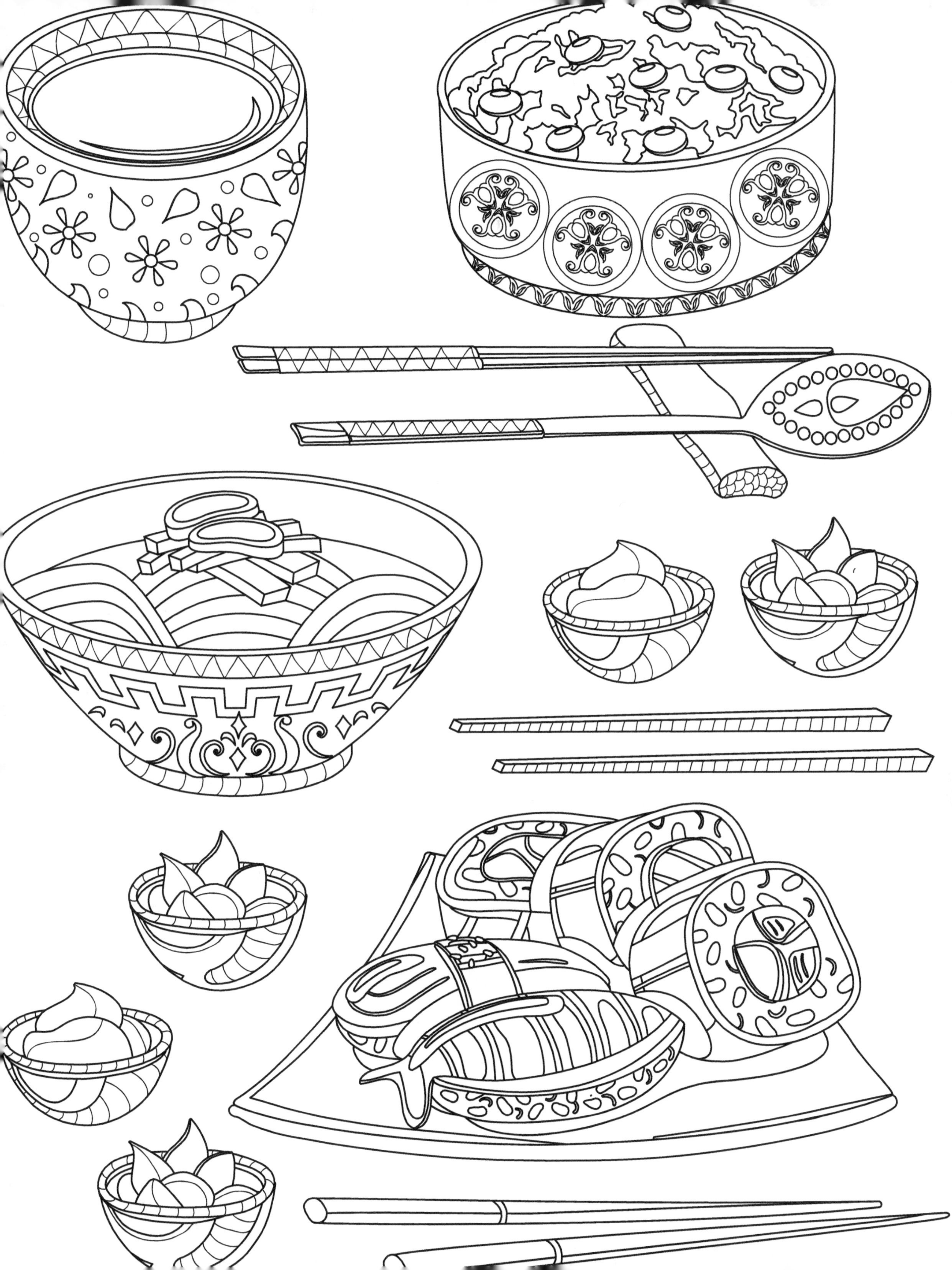

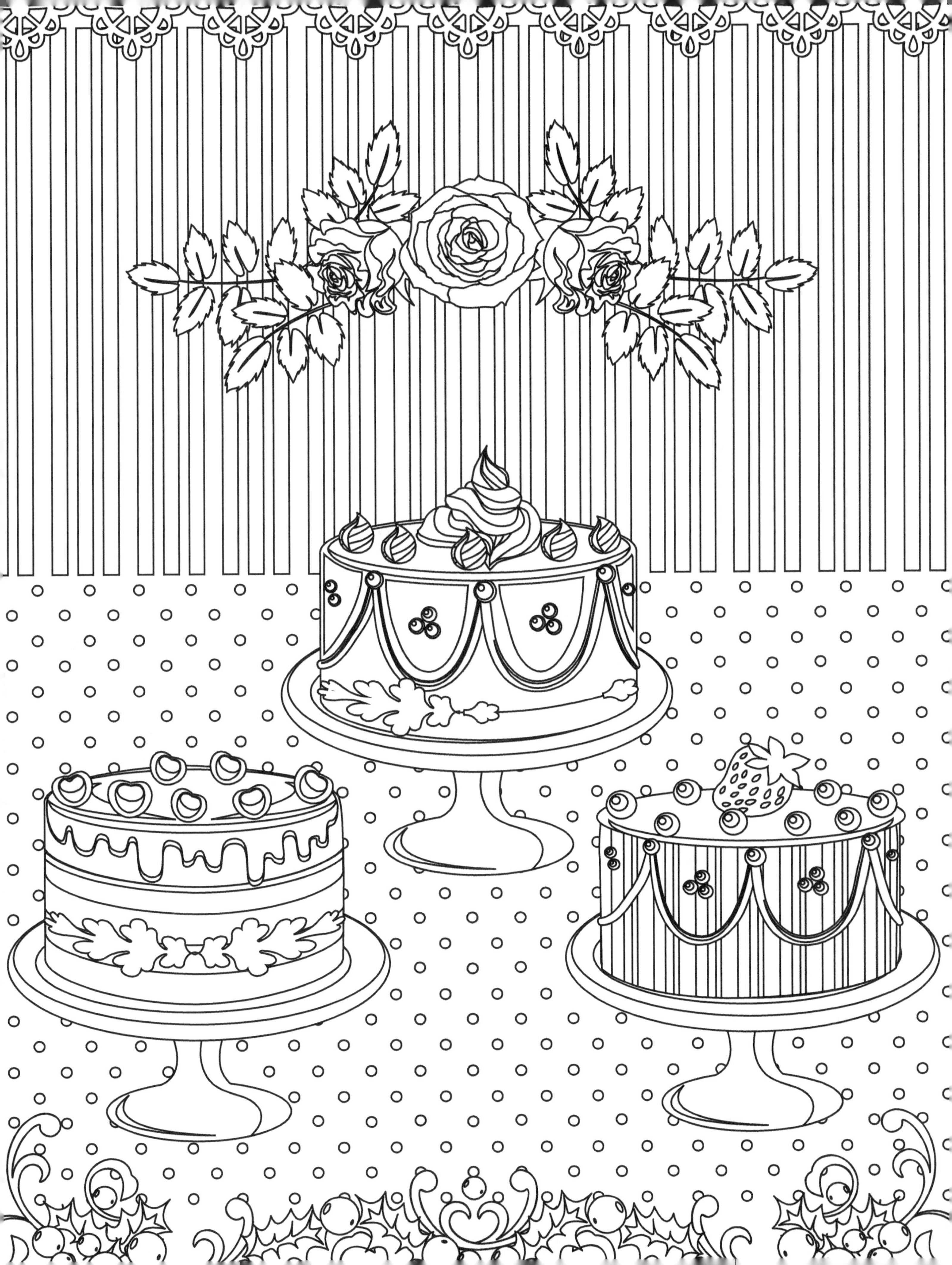

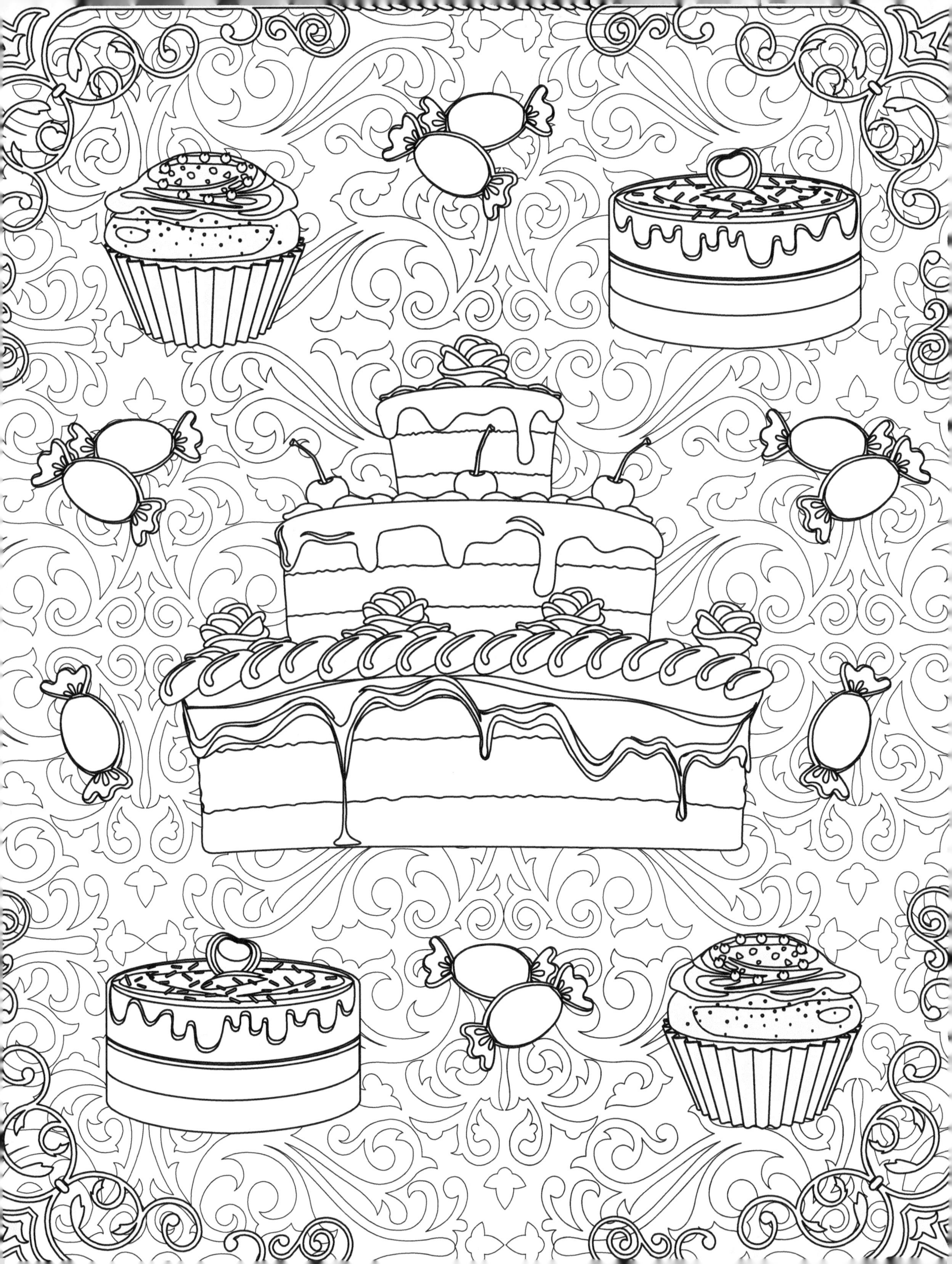

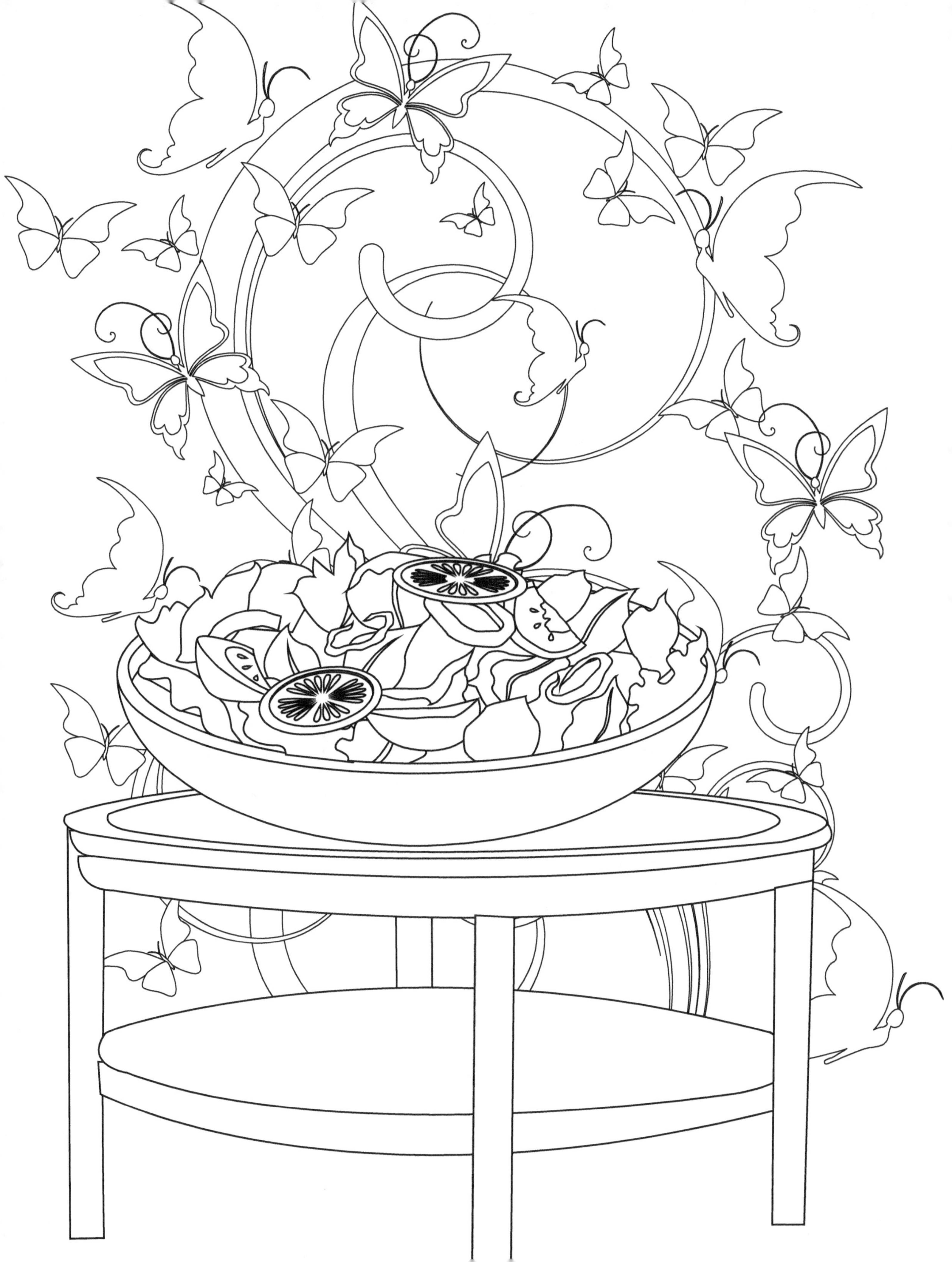

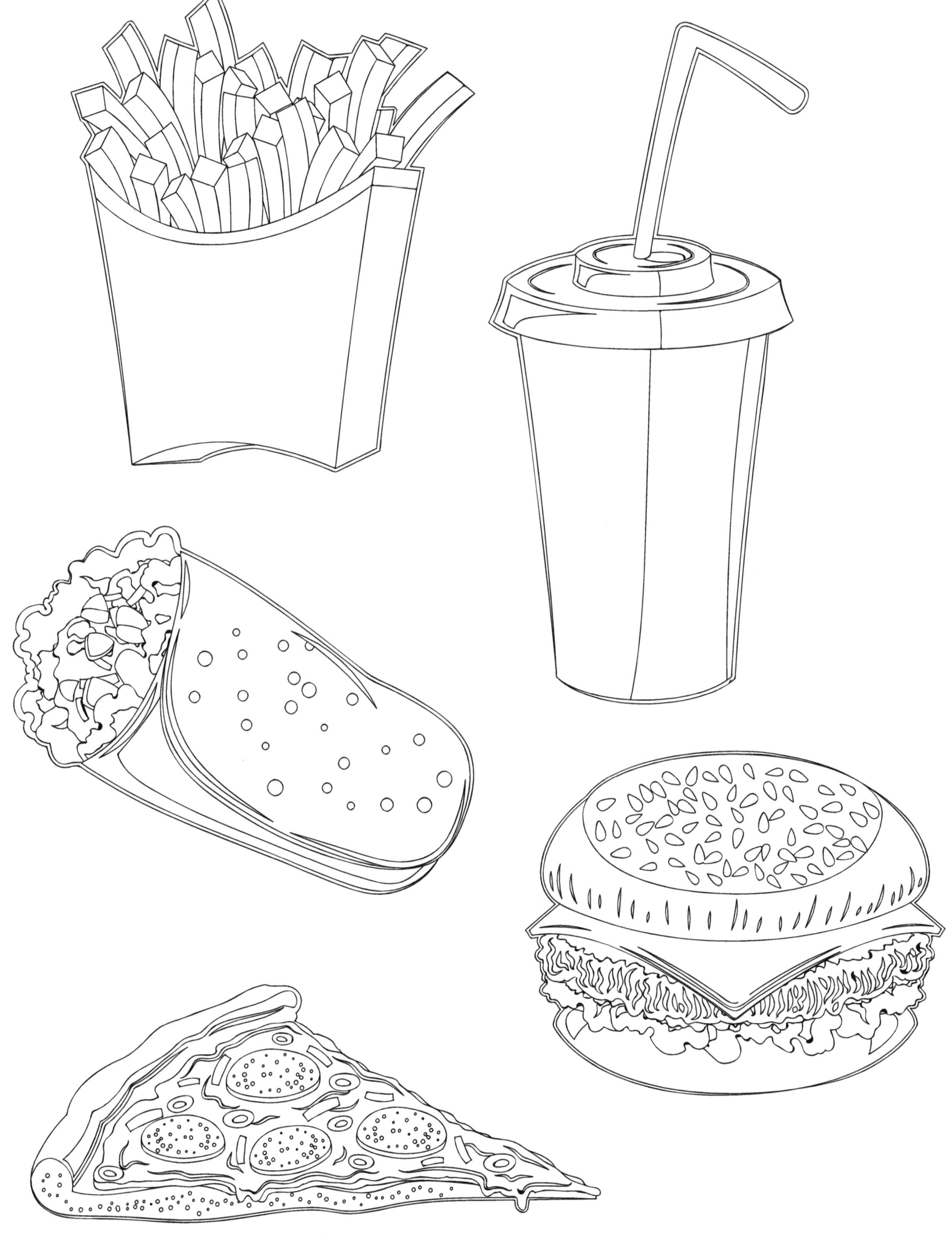

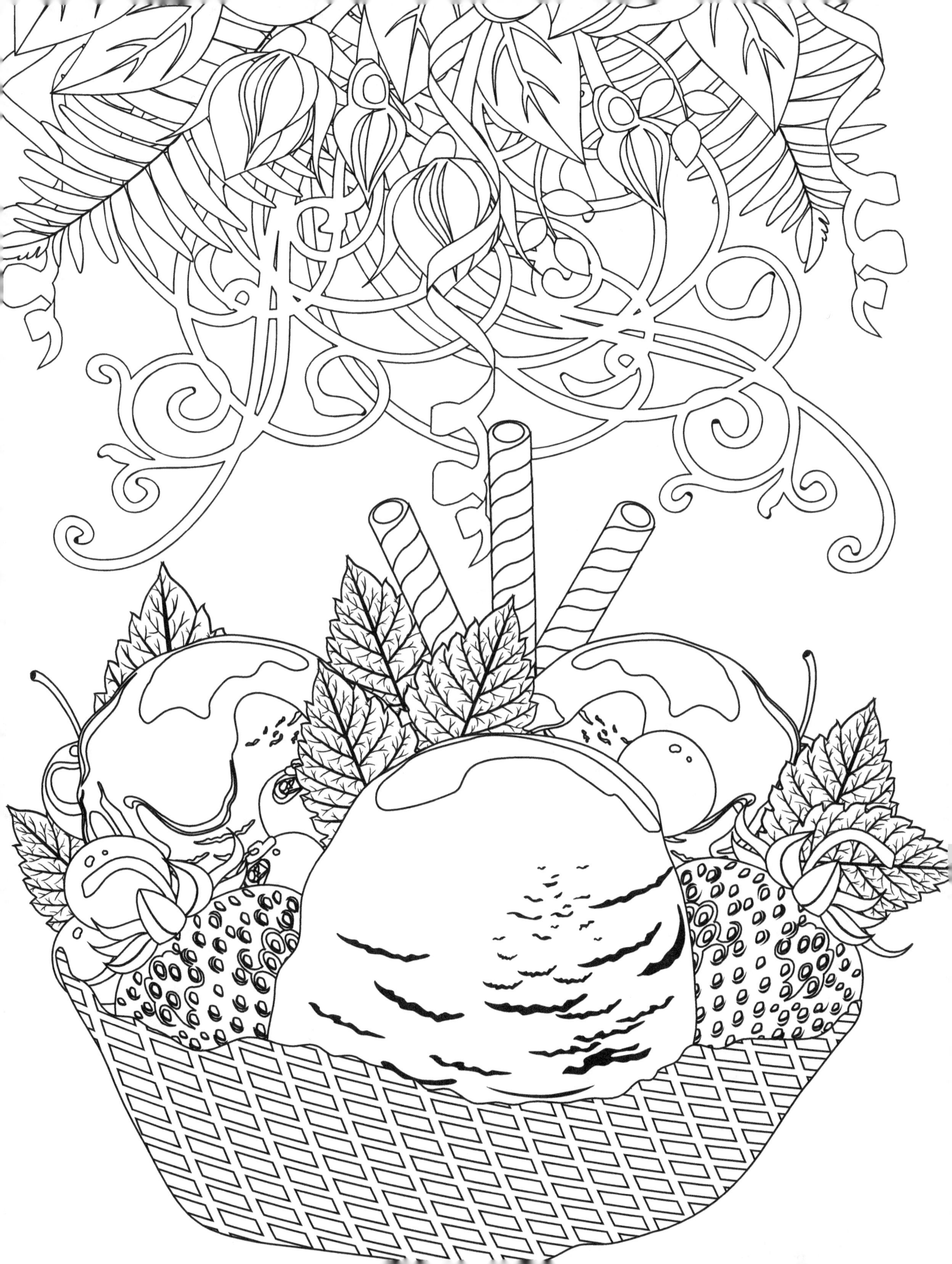

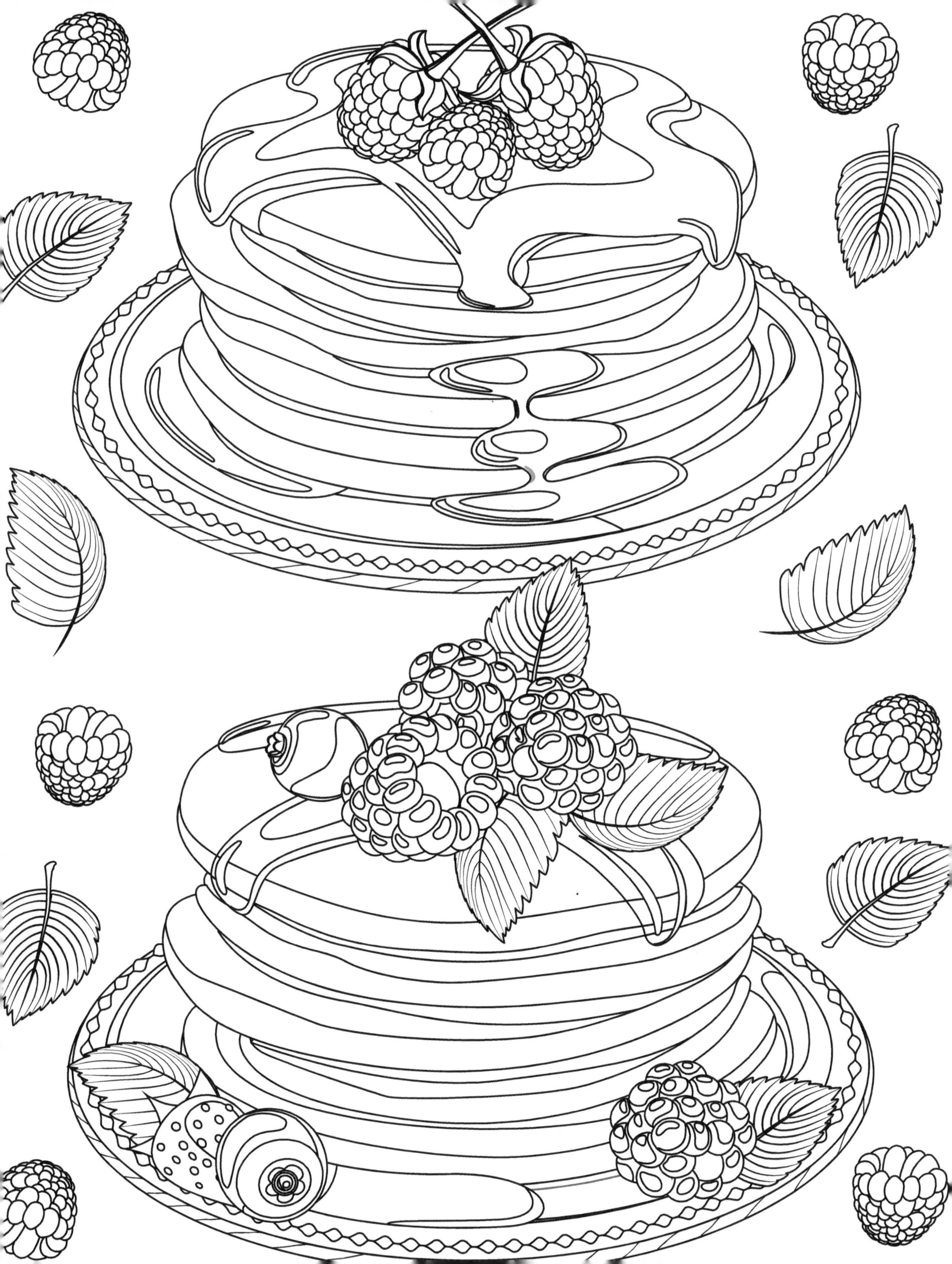

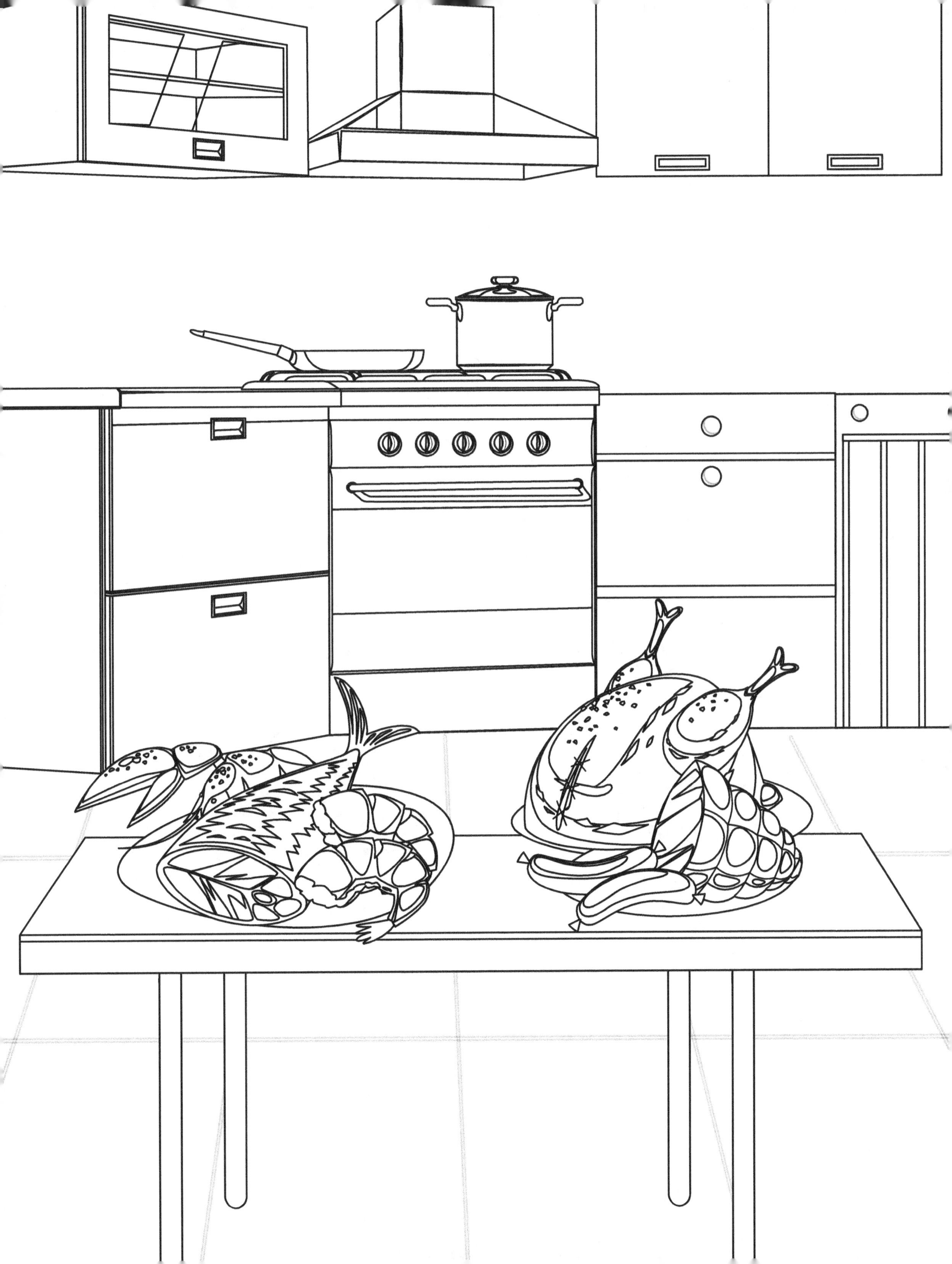

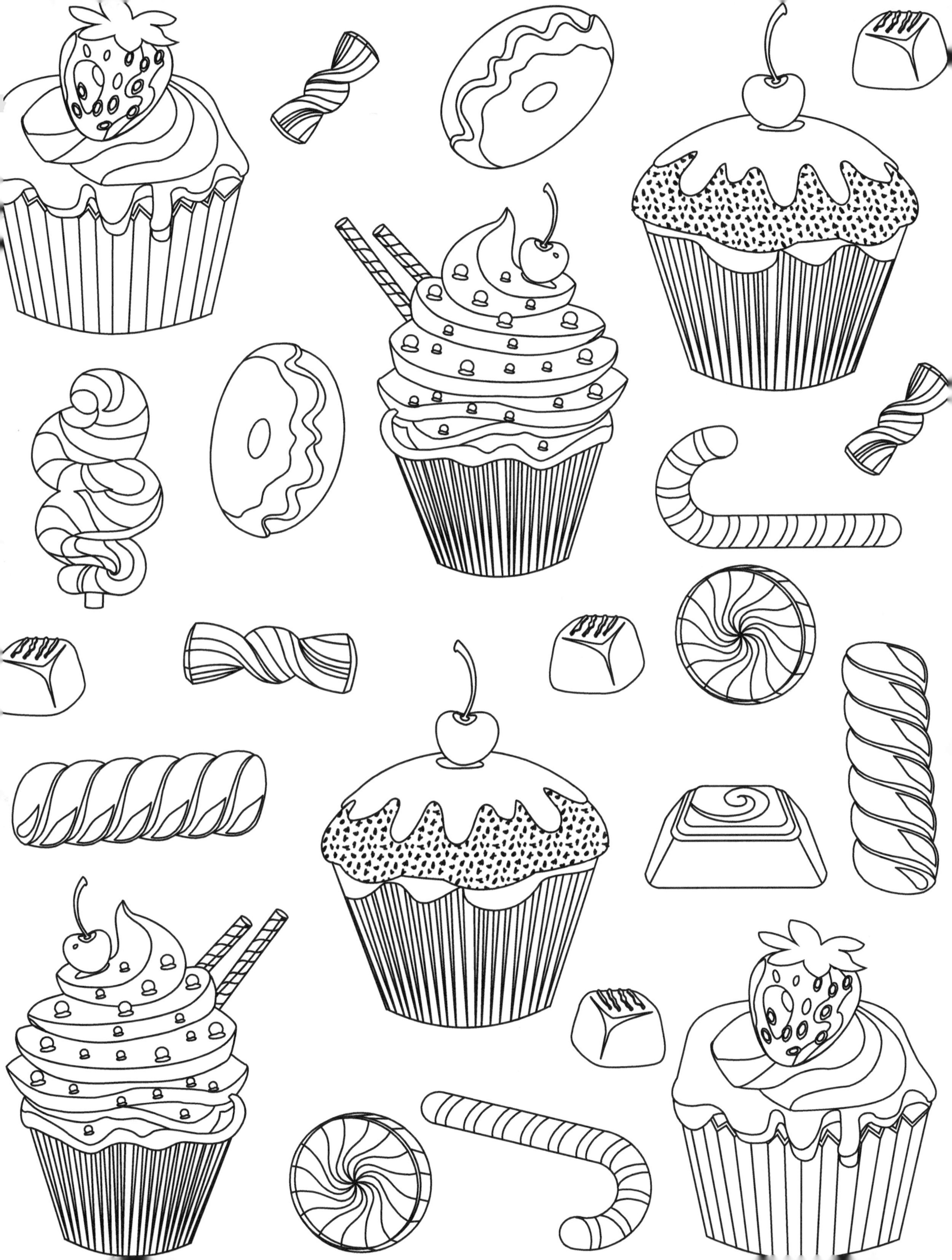

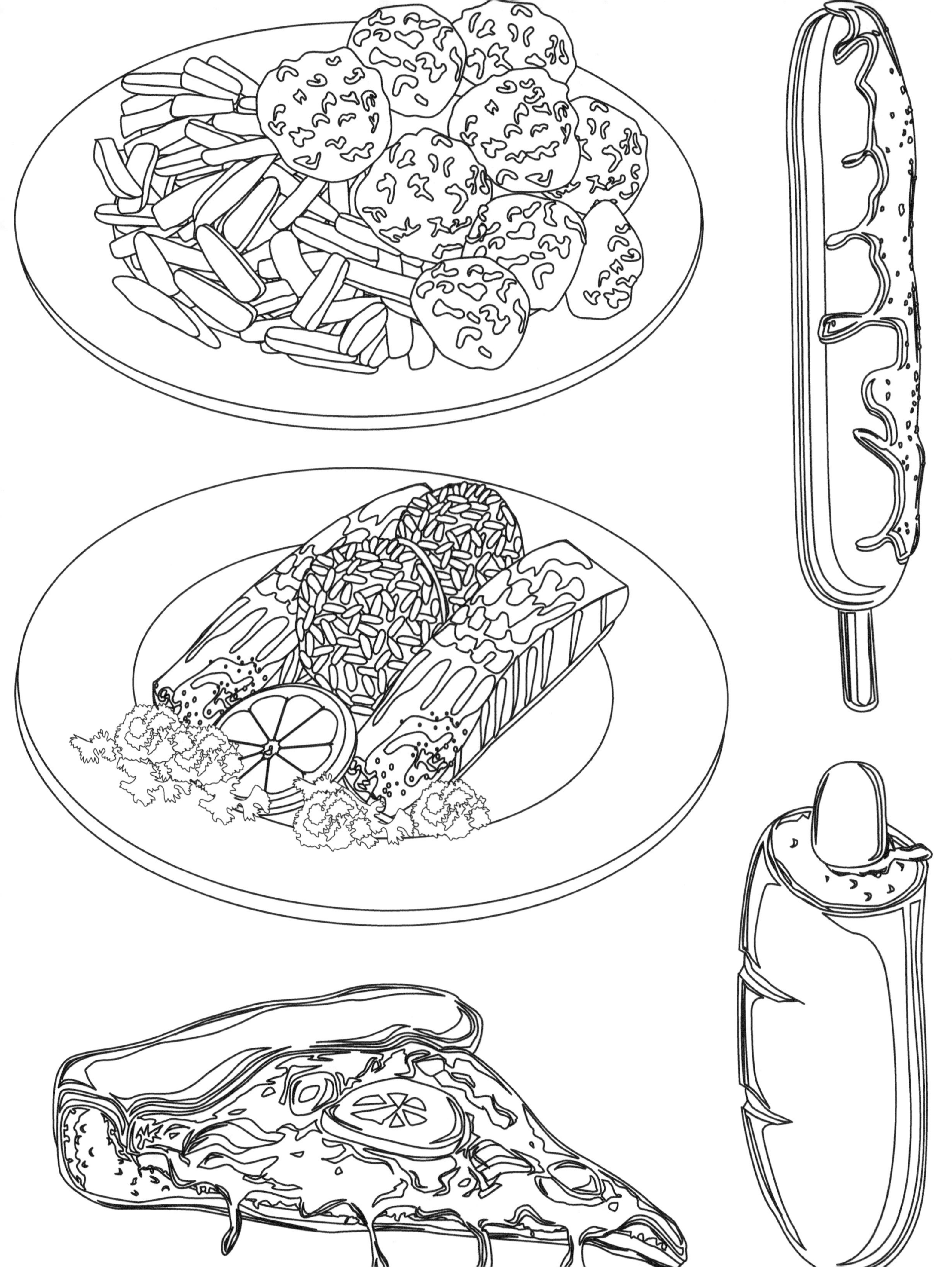

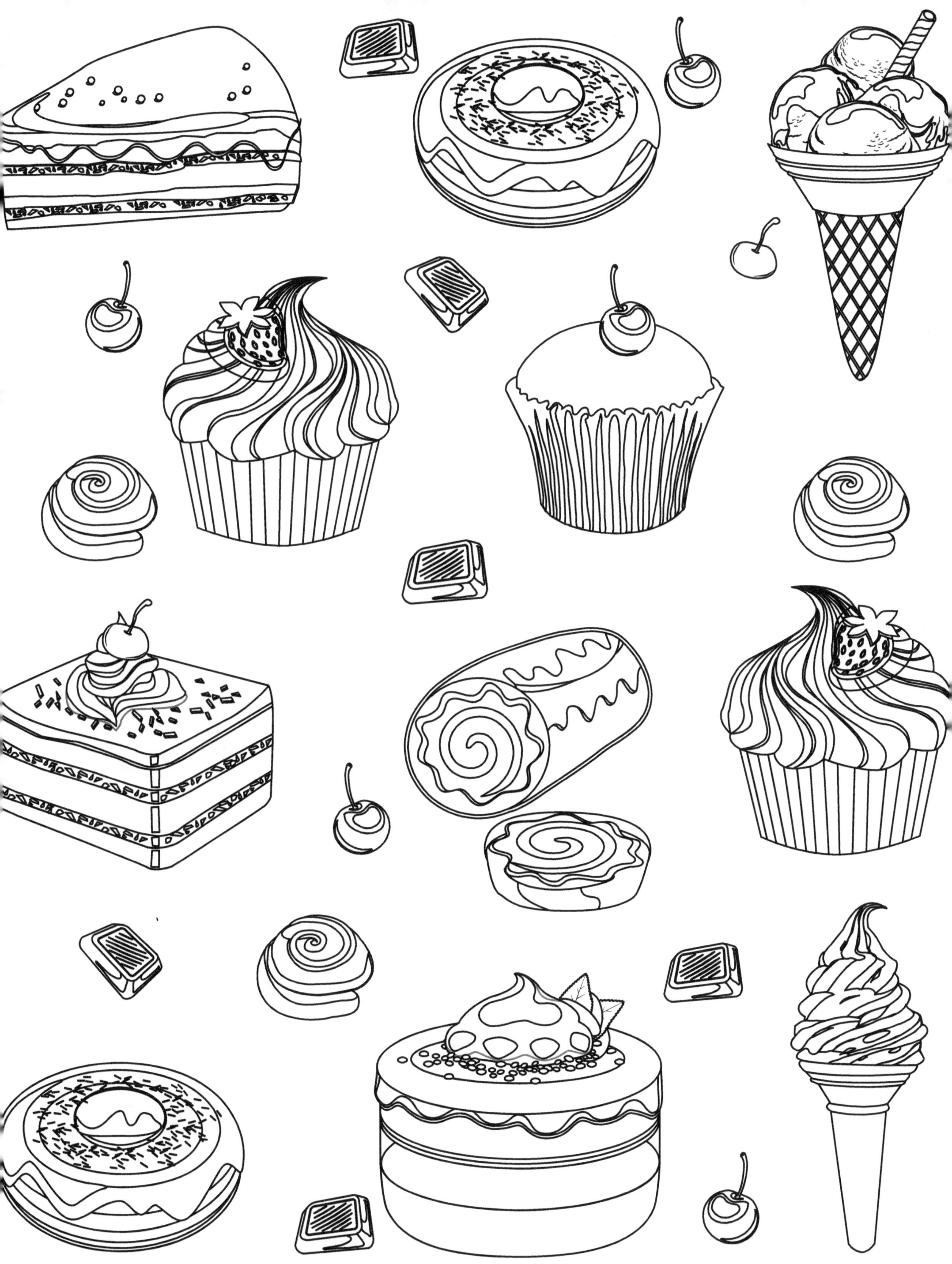

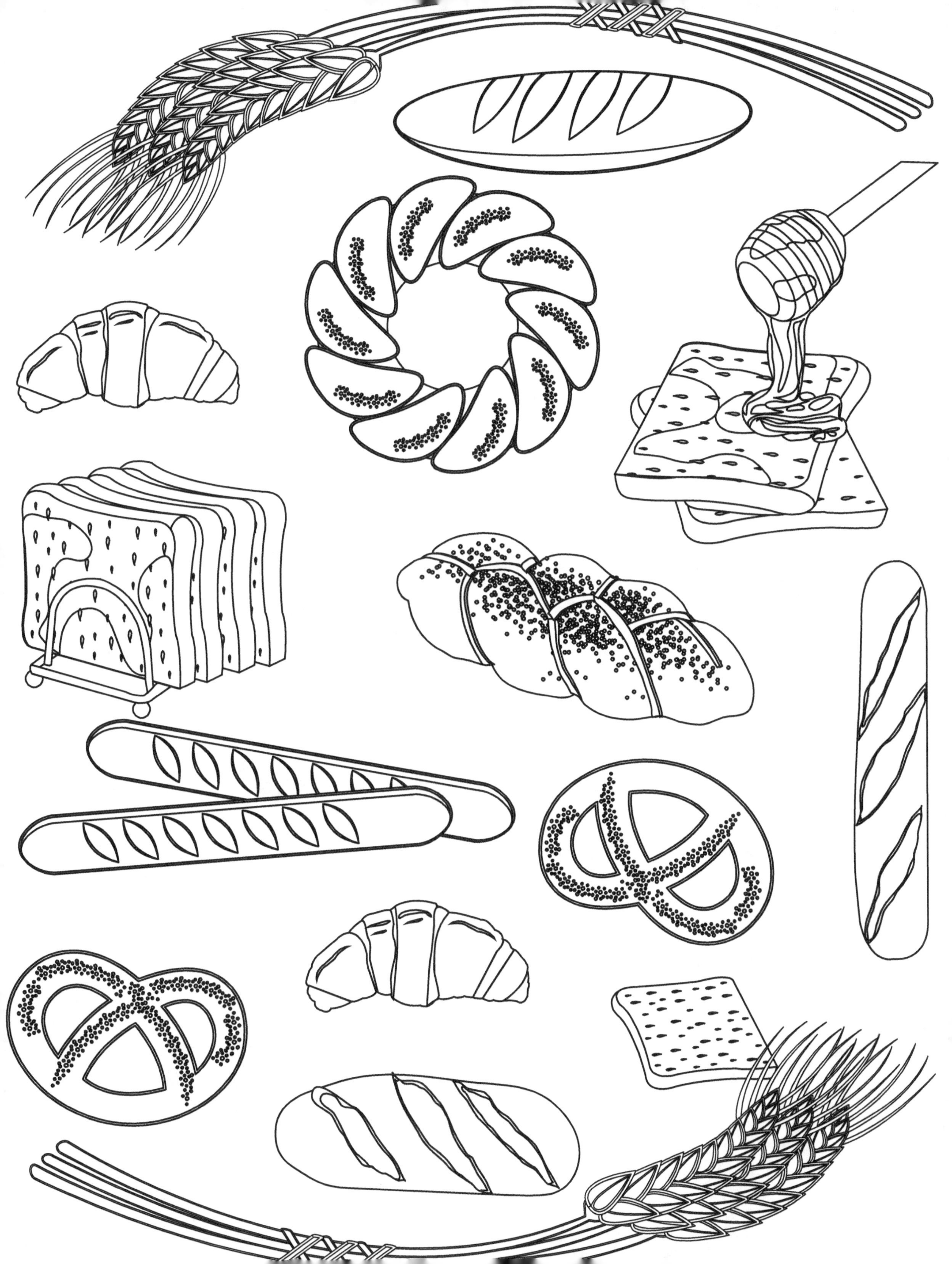

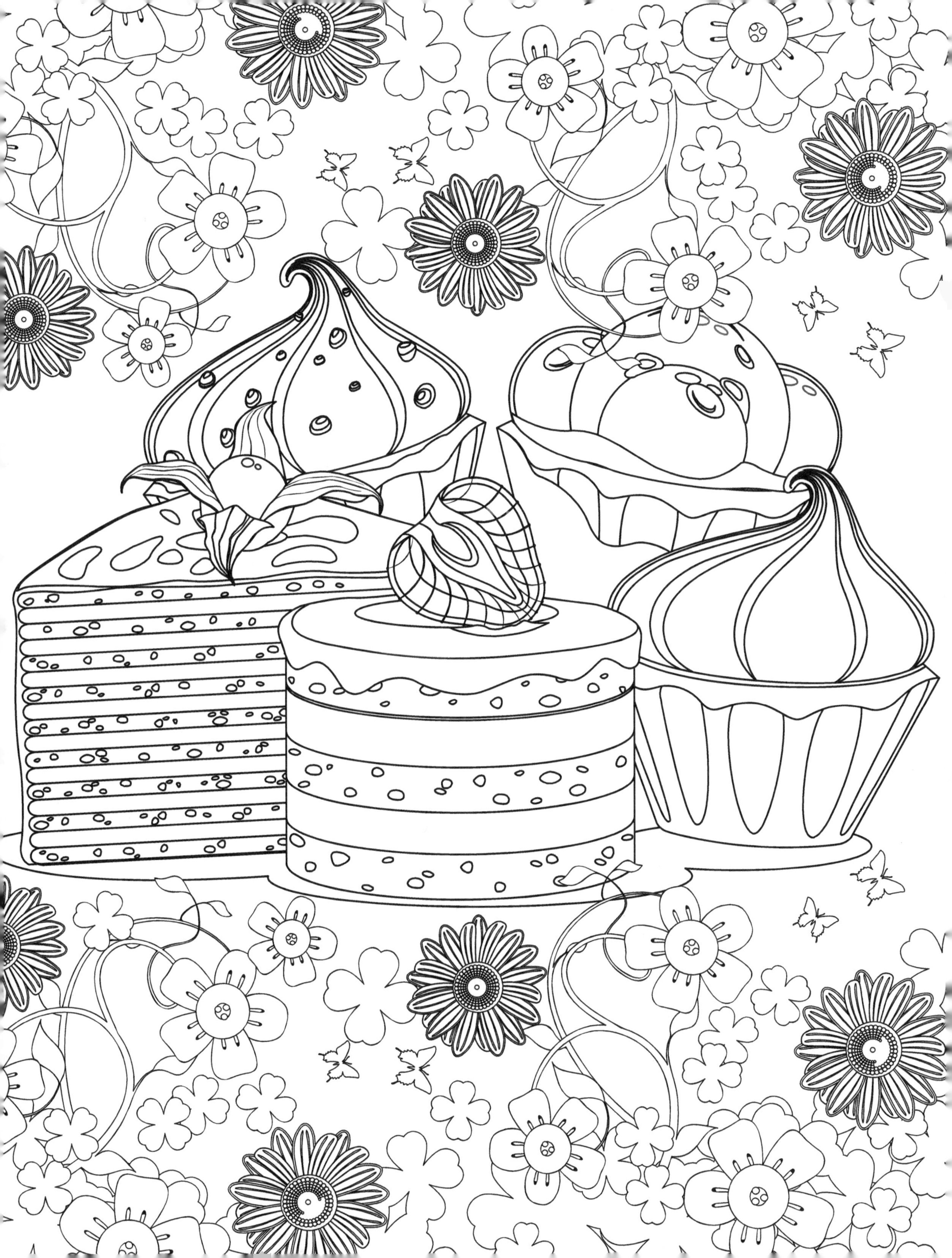

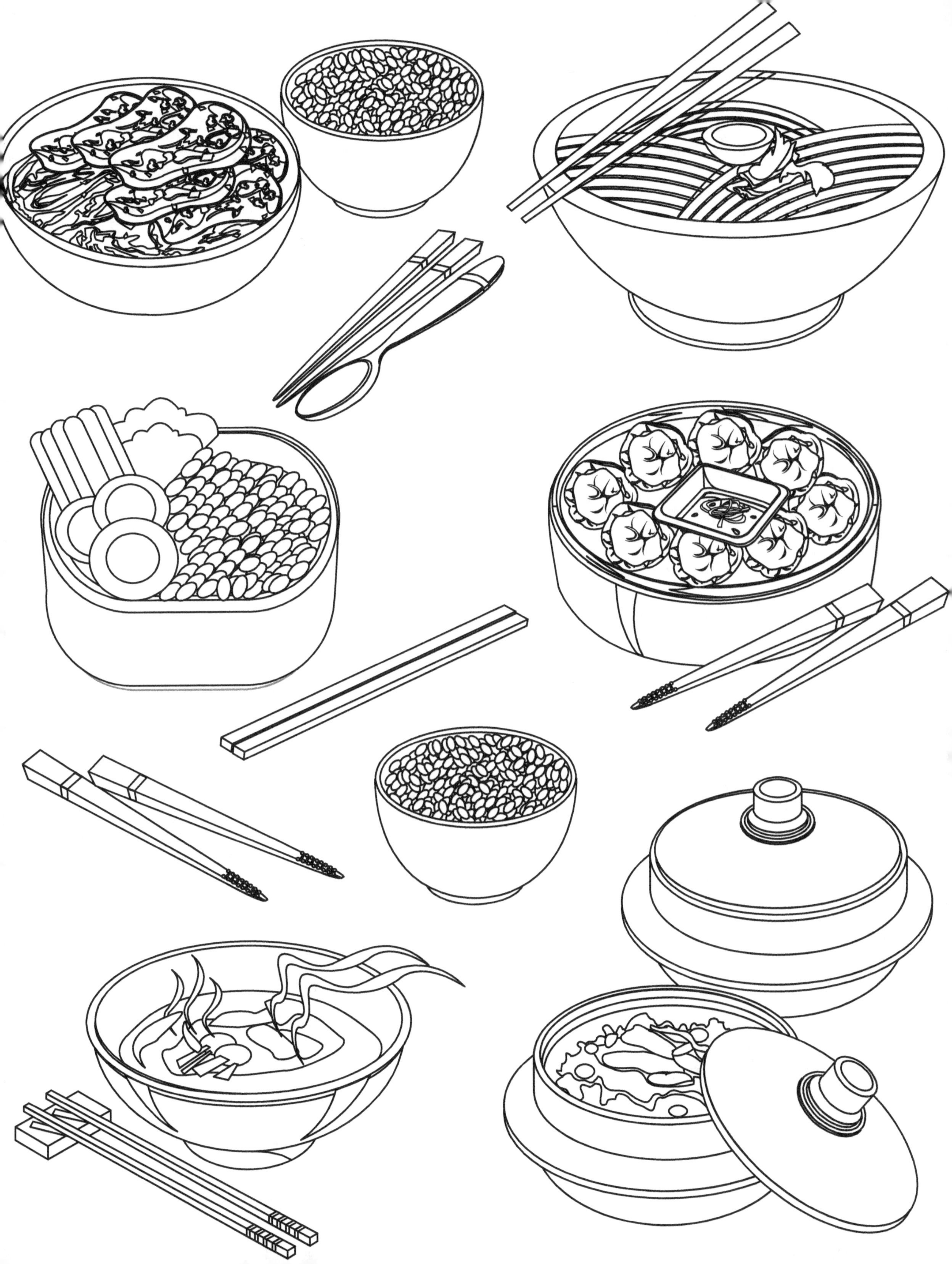

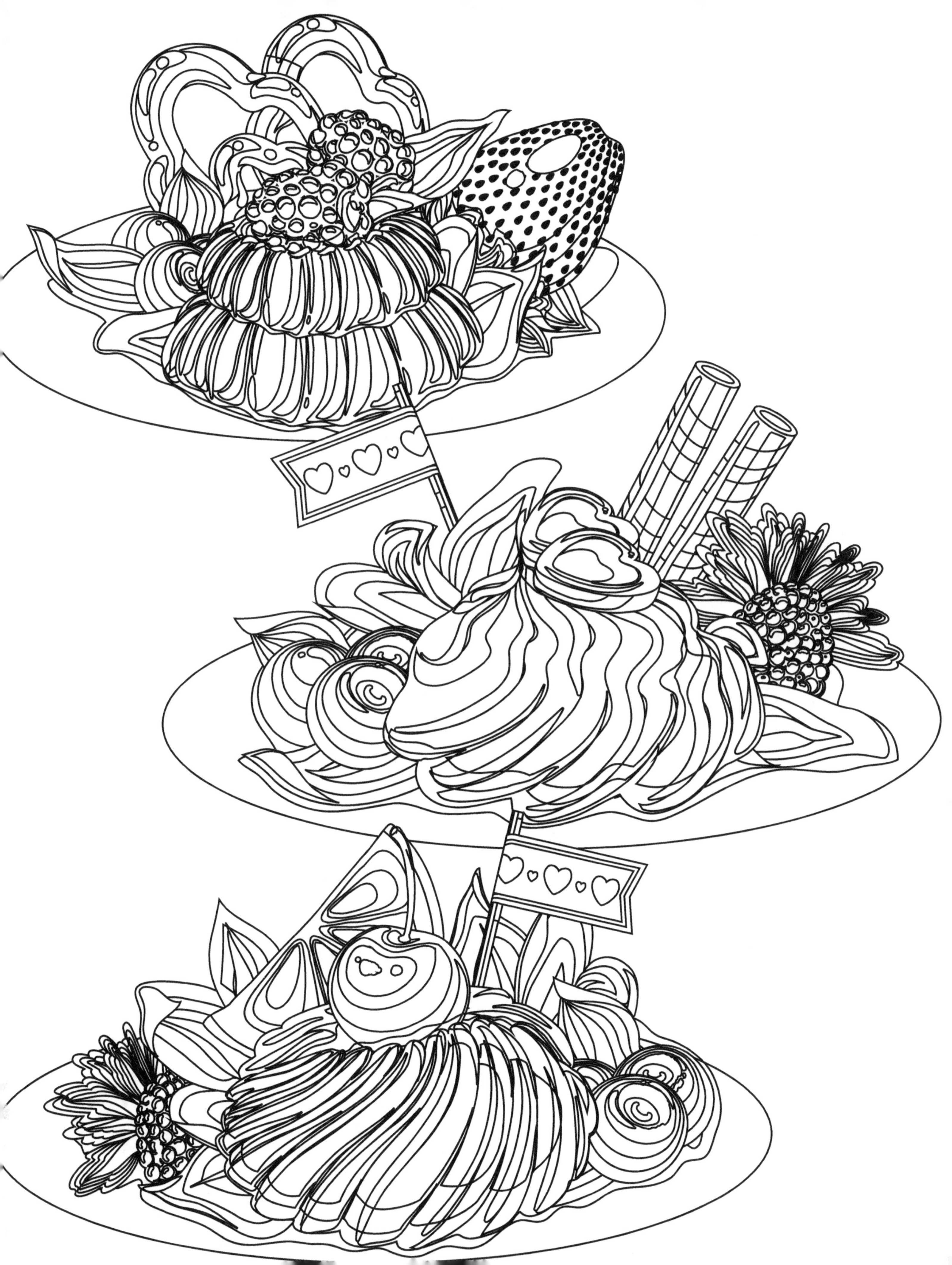

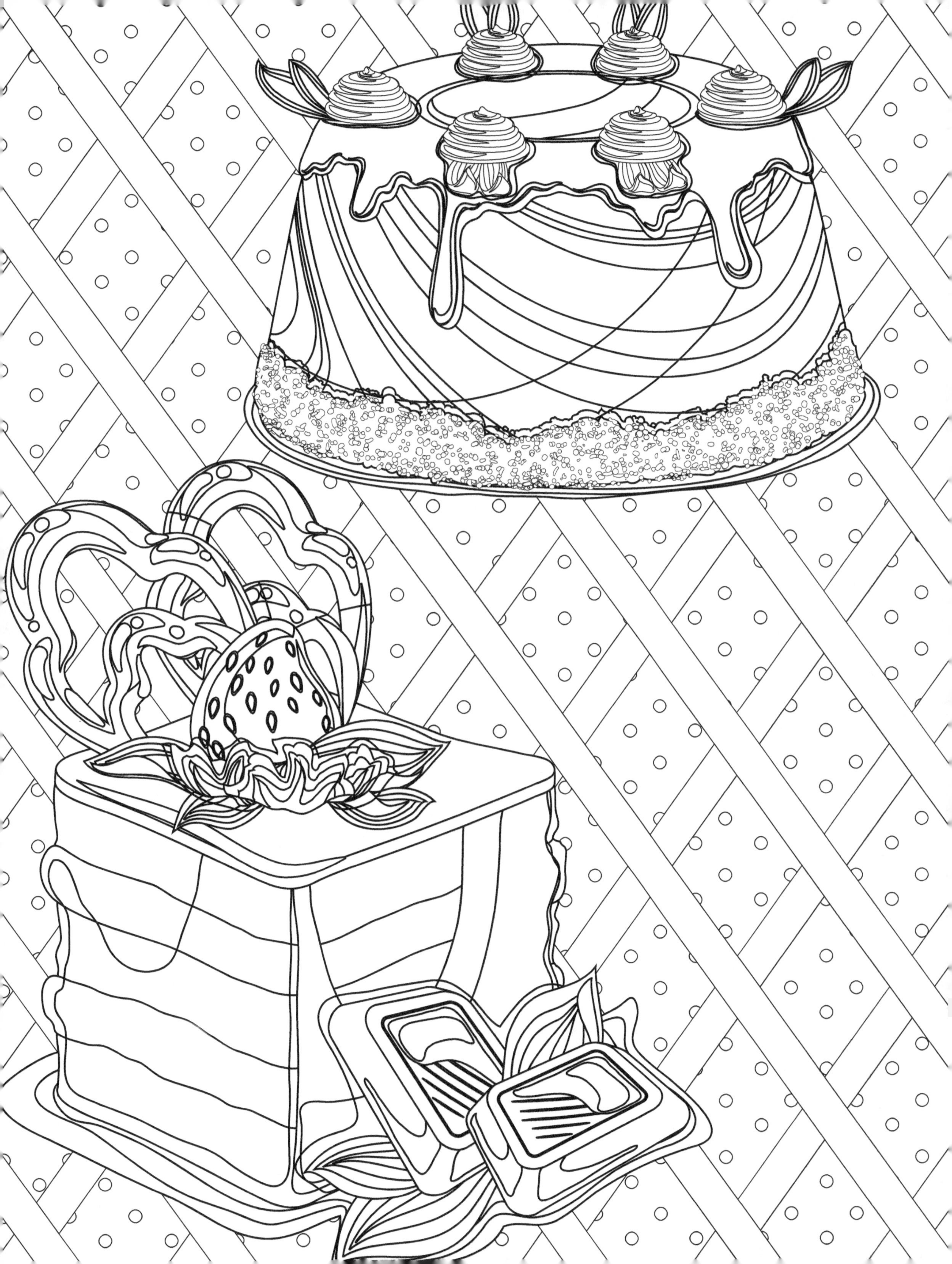

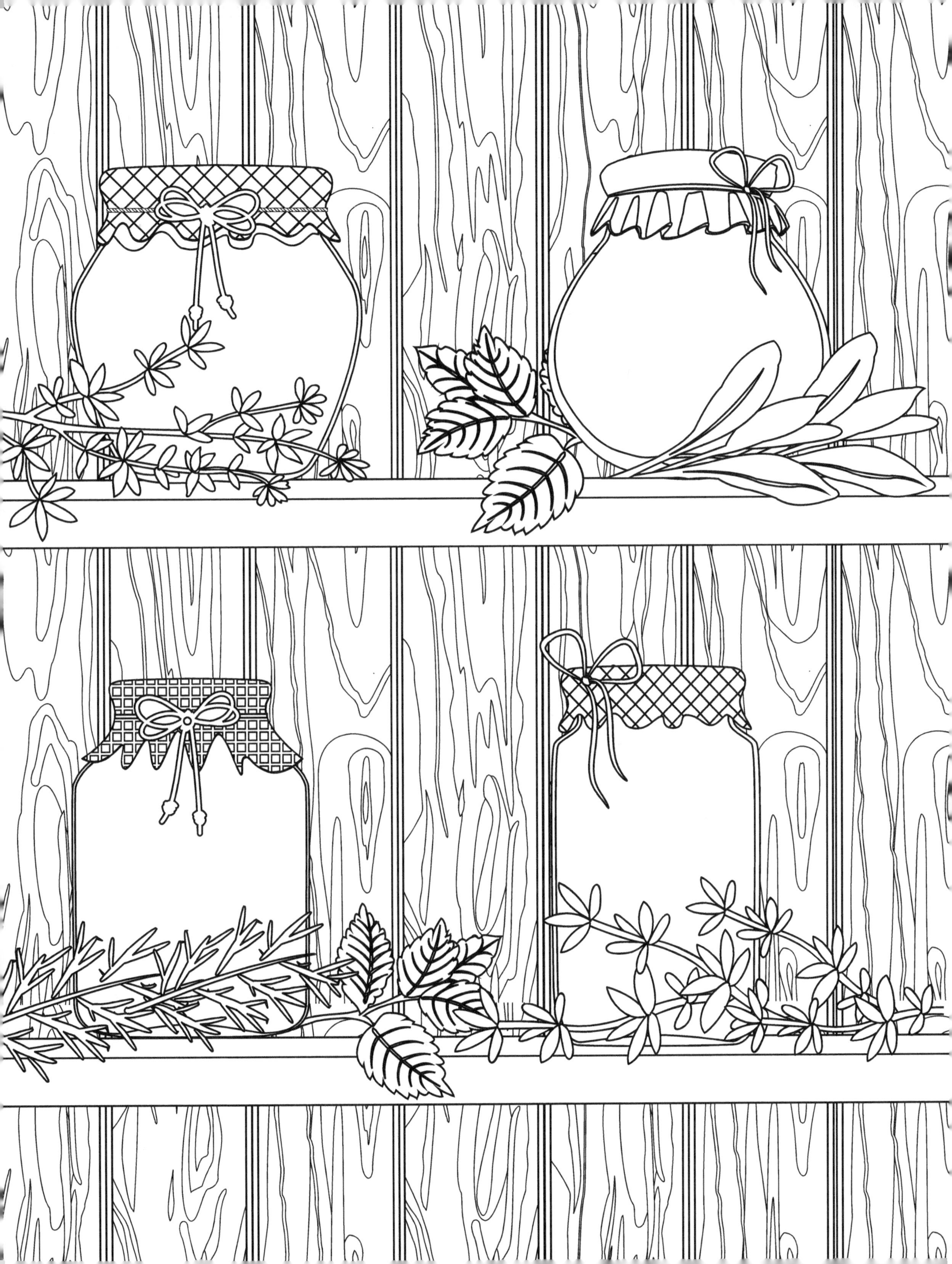

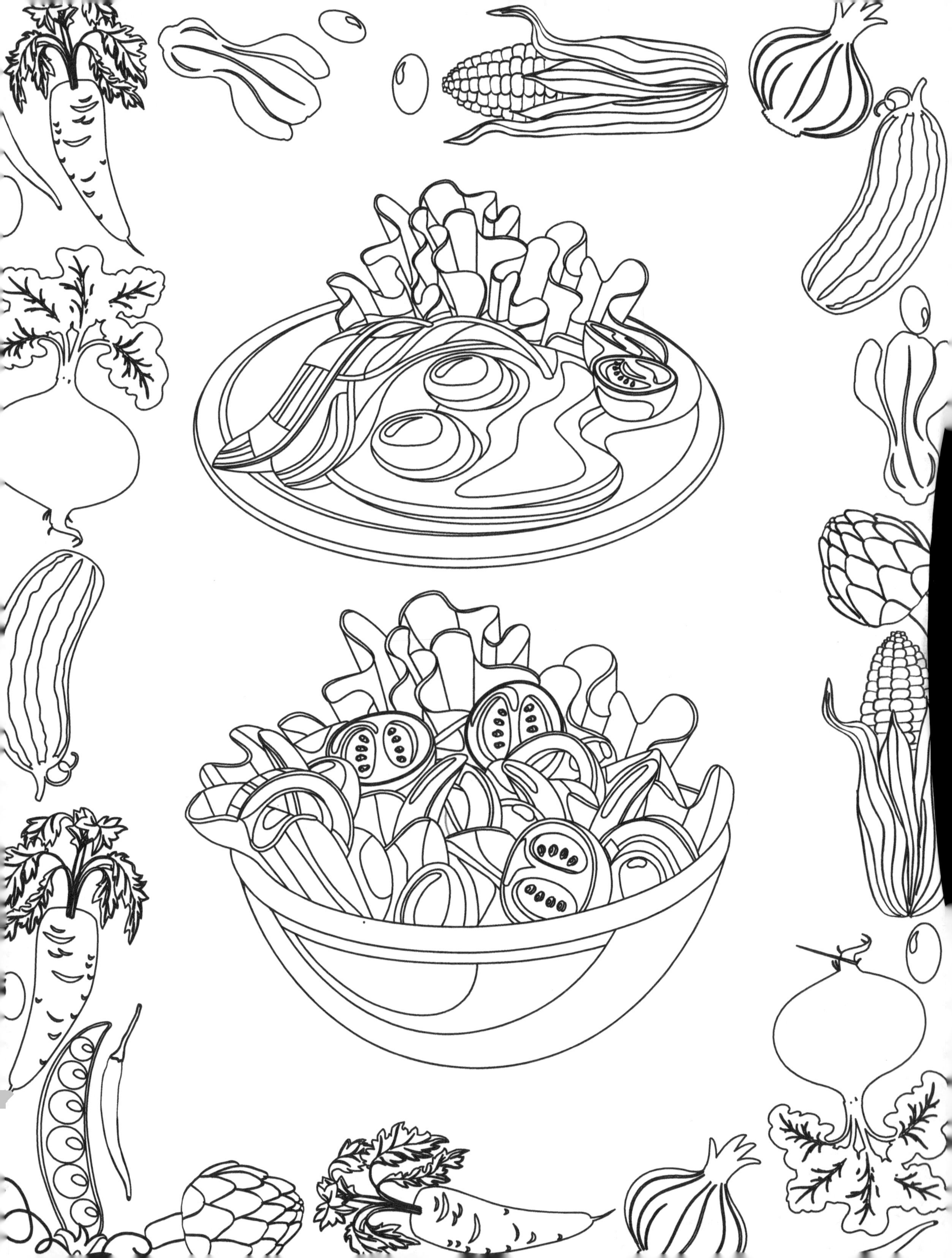